Crockery Pot Recipes

by
van kaatz

MAJOR BOOKS • CHATSWORTH, CALIFORNIA

DEDICATIONS

1. To the 20,000,000 crockery pot slow-cookers in the United States. May their numbers increase.

2. To Genevieve Stuttaford for saying nice things about *The Thrifty Gourmet's Chicken Cook Book*.

3. To Helen Worth, author of prize winning cook books and director of New York's oldest gourmet cooking school, for saying nice things about *The Thrifty Gourmet's Chicken Cook Book* —and in hope that this book will convince her that crockery pot slow-cookers have a definite part to play in American hot cuisine.

4. To our neighbors in the 10600 block on Saloma Avenue in Mission Hills, California— especially Joyce Gordon and Anita Liebe—for numerous recipe suggestions and enthusiastic tasting services.

5. And, but not least, to you who bought this book. May it bring you enjoyment.

CONTENTS

INTRODUCTION

When I first read about crockery cooking in a popular women's magazine (I get a lot of good ideas from them), I realized at once that it was a new application of the old and matchless principle of slow-cooking; an electrified casserole that could be a boon to working wives and to working singles —male or female—who live alone. It could free them from the frantic rush of trying to put a meal together after returning home tired from a hard day at the office. What could be easier than putting together the ingredients for a hot main dish in the morning, plugging in the slow-cooker, and leaving dinner to cook unattended for the whole day—returning in the evening to lift the lid on a savory, delicious repast!

And it is inexpensive also. You can cook all day for about what it takes to operate a 75-watt bulb.

Slow cooking . . . long, slow cooking . . . long, slow cooking without ever lifting the lid. . . . My mouth watered for beans baked for a day and a night until they burst with flavor; for soups that taste as if they had been cooked in a giant pot on the back of an old iron, wood-burning stove for days. These were things I absolutely could not prepare with any kitchen appliance we owned. I threw down the magazine and announced to Mary Lou-My-Wife that I was about to dash out to the neighborhood discount house and buy us the best crockery pot slow-cooker there is.

Then, before she could interject her usual "But, Van . . . ," I romanced her a little to strengthen my position. In my best Shakespearean manner and orotund tones I added: "And I shall prepare for you with this wondrous vessel such gustatory triumphs as will make you fair swoon with their delights. Then, whilst they seethe and simmer to a special goodness, we shall steal away with our stripling son fondly called Benjie to walk among the beauties of nature and restore our wonder. For 'I know a place where on the wild thyme blows, where oxlips and the nodding violet grows.' Then, in the cool of the even-time we will return to our abode and discover a most toothsome and savory feast awaiting—all hot and savory . . . ambrosial . . . gustable . . . nectareous. . . ."

"Oh, sire," she interrupted, also falling into the Elizabethan language of The Bard, "'a woman would run through fire and water for such a kind heart' to quote *The Merry Wives of Windsor.*" Then she reverted to colloquial speech: "We liberated women don't have to be wooed and coaxed all the time. You hit the right argument when you said you'd do the cooking yourself in this newfangled pot. Don't forget, I already have the burner-with-the-brain, my pressure cooker, and all those speedy appliances you've already bought me. To say nothing of the phone numbers of several home delivery food services. So, I think it's okay for you to buy yourself a kitchen tool. But, what will you make with this slow-cooker that you can't with some pot we already have?"

"Well," said I, "there's a *cassoulet*—the domestic version, or *Toulousain*, or *de Castelnaudary* —or beans slow-baked in beer . . . or *Cholent* . . ."

"What's *Cholent?*" she questioned.

"Aha!" I cried. "See what convenience foods and fast-cooking have done! You have forgotten your ethnic heritage. We who cherish memories of a Jewish home and mother—and father—recall the wonderful foods with which the table was loaded. Right up at the top of the list . . . right after the chicken soup and the chopped liver . . . was *Cholent*. Or maybe your folks called it *Shulent*, or perhaps *Shalet*. The way our people pronounce it depends on what part of Europe your forefathers and foremothers left in a hurry— whether they were *Litvak*, or *Galitzianer*, *Roumainische*, or *Deutschische*.

"Heinrich Heine, the great Jewish-German poet, sang its praises in his poem, 'Princess Sabbath':

> *There shall steam for thee a dish*
> *That in very truth divine is—*
> *Thou shalt eat today of Shalet!*

"It's a one-dish meal that Jews invented long ago in order to have a hot meal on holidays and on the Sabbath, when cooking is prohibited. Ingredients differ according to regional origin, but it's usually meat, beans, barley, and seasonings. The method is always the same, though, long slow cooking at a low temperature.

11

"I recall reading that, in the European ghettos, families delivered their individual, covered pots of *Cholent* to the local bakeries, and just before sundown on Friday—when the bake-oven fires were allowed to die down for the Sabbath—the pots were put into the ovens, to cook on stored heat until they were reclaimed after the final service on Saturday night. Then they were wrapped in cloths and carried home—all hot and ready to eat. Now, if that's not the same slow-cooking as this crockery pot idea, which is a lot easier, I will eat it *and* the pot!

"Surely," she said, "but don't forget that other civilizations have gone in for slow-cooking. The Greeks, for instance. And what would a New England shore dinner be without a steaming fire-pit? Or what about the Dutch ovens they used to bury under the coals of the cooking fires out on the Western prairies?"

"Right on," I cheered. "So, now that we're agreed I'm going out to buy a crockery pot slow-cooker."

"I'll go along with that," she said. And she did, too: went along. I'm still not sure which of us made the decision to buy the pot we're both using.

Notice, I said "both." I didn't talk her into this, haven't been able to talk her into anything since the night I proposed. Marriage, that is. I knew, however, that she would not leave the cooker alone, just as surely as she knew I wanted to try it out. Maybe she realized it would provide material for my third cook book before I did.

Probably it would be truer to say "our" third cook book. When I started out as The Thrifty Gourmet, for the *Chopped Meat Cook Book*, she was helpful; even more so on the *Chicken Cook*

12

Book—with ideas for improvements, with polishing, typing and proofreading. I shall probably never be sorry I married an editor. But she was most helpful with *Crockery Pot Recipes,* as a long spell of illness kept me from actively participating in the testing procedures and she had to test countless recipes and discuss them with me before we selected those that have gone into the book.

There was much to learn. The literature on the crockery pot is contradictory and we had to experiment to discover its limitations as well as its advantages.

We think it has tremendous potential as a slow-cooking appliance and can be put to good use for short-time cookery as well—as a chafing dish, for instance, or a fondue pot, or a bun warmer. We intend to go right on developing new recipes for it long after this book is in print.

Both of us believe you will enjoy using your crockery pot slow-cooker if you follow the hints and cautions in the next chapter—and each dish you cook will be full of flavors you have never tasted before, even if you have used the same combinations of ingredients and cooked them another way.

—THE THRIFTY GOURMET
(Van and Mary Lou Kaatz)
September, 1975

CHAPTER ONE
HELPFUL HINTS AND CAUTIONS

As with every other new appliance or tool, there is a necessary learning period that must be endured. But when this familiarization phase is past, the master (or mistress) of the crockery pot slow-cooker experiences a pleasurable pride in the ability to create repasts which delight family and guests—at economical prices and with all the goodness and vitamins intact—that makes the apprenticeship all worthwhile.

A good part of the enjoyment of the crockery pot is the new freedom: being free of the kitchen all day while dinner cooks itself unwatched—even for a day and a night if required. You're free to go off to work, to go shopping, to do the million-and-one things you have to do every day and yet produce meals of gourmet quality, appearance, and taste.

READ THE MANUFACTURER'S INSTRUCTIONS FIRST

Read the instruction booklet that came with your crockery pot all the way through—at least 3 times. Commit its do's and don't's to memory. There are injunctions in it which apply only to your special make of pot, which might make all the difference between success or failure. Become especially familiar with your control settings. Some cookers have special browning cycles at very high heat and you must be sure to re-set them after browning to the HIGH or LOW setting which suits your recipe. Others have thermostatic controls which must be set to the Fahrenheit (or Celsius) equivalent of HIGH or LOW, and set exactly or it will make a significant difference in cooking time.

I can attest to that. I—or Mary Lou-My-Wife—have already done all the dumb things you can do with a slow-cooker. Like plugging it in and then forgetting to set the control. We went away for the day and returned to find the cooker still set on OFF and our dinner as raw as when we left. I said that she did it. She said I had done it. Then we went out to a very expensive restaurant for dinner.

The next time something went wrong it was because one of us—no names, please—had set the control carefully to LOW, and then forgotten to plug in the cord! It was close to dinnertime when we discovered the error, but since it was a meat soup that couldn't be hurt by especially long cooking we plugged the crockery pot in, went out for dinner, and enjoyed the soup next night. I must say that I was not especially overjoyed by my wife's muttered remarks ("What kind of *thrifty* gourmet did I marry," etc.) when I had to borrow from her to pay the check.

But now we have both of our crockery pot slow-cookers well in hand and are turning out savory stews, soups, meat loaves, cakes—even yeast breads and souffles!—with only rare and minor failures. And from the experience gained through trial and error we offer you the advice that follows.

MOST RECIPES ARE FOR A
3½-QUART COOKER

Most of the recipes in this book are for the 3½-quart crockery pot cooker, which seems to be the most popular size. They will also work in most 4½-quart and 5-quart cookers without alteration. But if you have a cooker of smaller capacity than 3½ quarts you'll have to learn how to reduce quantities. This is easy, and your manufacturer's instruction book will give you details.

All of these recipes use either one or the other of two temperature settings: HIGH (300 degrees Fahrenheit, 149 degrees Celsius) or LOW (200 degrees Fahrenheit, 93 degrees Celsius). If your cooker has a continuous thermostatic control, set it *exactly* on the correct degree of heat or you may cook at too high or too low a temperature for good results. If your control shows only LOW, HIGH, and OFF, be sure to set it exactly on the indicated points, as there are no in-between settings and it may not cook at all. Also, be sure to consult the manufacturer's handbook for differentials in time for high-altitude operation.

For best results, your cooker should always be at least half-filled. And if you have any doubts about its true capacity, fill it with water and measure the contents. About ½-quart of space at the top cannot be used, so a 4½-quart cooker's useable capacity may only be 4 quarts. However, using this water measurement test, you may discover that your cooker actually holds 5 quarts—giving you 4½ quarts useable capacity.

I discovered this anomaly when I bought our second cooker. It was rated as a 5-quart pot by the maker of our 4½-quart model, but standing there side by side they looked absolutely identical in capacity. So, not trusting my bifocals, I measured both units and found no significant variations in dimensions. Then I filled them with liquid and discovered they had identical capacities. So much for manufacturers' claims.

The only real advantage that the second pot offers over the first is that the crockery liner comes out for cleaning, or for storage of its contents in the refrigerator. This is worthwhile in itself. There is no need to claim greater capacity for it.

BROWNING IS NOT REQUIRED
FOR MEATS . . .

If the meat you cook in your crockery pot slow-cooker is relatively lean and well-trimmed, browning beforehand is not essential to the cooking process. However, there is much to be said for a pot roast or stew that is appetizingly colored as well as seasoned, therefore you may find that some type of browning is advisable for esthetic reasons.

BUT, IF YOU WANT TO BROWN . . .

I'm old-fashioned and like to brown meats in a heavy skillet before putting them into the crockery pot. Usually, I use fat, oil, butter, or some other shortening to brown the meat on all sides. Sometimes, I dice half a carrot and half an onion in about 2 tablespoons of fat, then add a tablespoon of sugar and stir and cook until the sugar carmelizes. This mixture I add to the browned meat in the crockery pot as a flavoring and coloring agent. You can get almost the same effect by adding Kitchen Bouquet, Gravy Master, or some other commercial browning agent that contains sugar and caramel.

There's another commercial browning agent

called Brown-Quick that I was introduced to by Helen Worth, who is a sort of distant relative of mine and author of such prizewinning cook books as *Hostess Without Help, Cooking Without Recipes,* and *Damyankee in a Southern Kitchen.* She developed it in her New York cooking school and it is becoming more and more available at good stores nationally. It can be used as a marinade, or to brown meat by brushing all surfaces with it before frying, roasting or broiling without extra fat. Or brush Brown-Quick on the meat in the crockery pot and forego preliminary browning in a skillet. This can also be done with the other browning agents previously mentioned, but Brown-Quick has no caramel or sugar in it, so it imparts a flavor that is different. It contains soy sauce, spices, and flavorings—including the very faintest whiff of garlic, which is a definite advantage.

Which brings up another caution: Using browning agents means you must adjust your seasonings somewhat. Otherwise you may end up with a dish too sweet, salty, spicy, or vinegary. Read the contents information on the label. Incidentally, you'll note that many competitive national brands are almost identical in composition!

USE A TRIVET UNDER THE MEATS

A metal meat rack (trivet), made either of perforated sheet steel or bent steel wire, will keep the meat from soaking up too much fat or stewing soggily in the juices at the bottom of the pot. If your cooker didn't come with a trivet, perhaps the manufacturer offers one as an accessory by mail order. Otherwise, you ought to be able to get one that fits closely from your local hardware store or gourmet utensil shop.

21

MEAT GENERALLY COOKS QUICKER THAN THE VEGETABLES

Vegetables should be quartered or diced, and put at the bottom and sides of your crockery cooker. Carrots should be placed well down into the liquid. Young vegetables cook faster than old ones, but some do not take to slow cooking and should be added later or cooked separately and added to the serving platter. Check the handbook with the cooker for cooking information about vegetables, as there's variation from make to make. This separate cooking has another advantage—it will prevent such culinary fiascoes as sickly pale purple potatoes in your *Boeuf Bourguignonne*.

Pastas, rice, seafood, and milk should be added later—not cooked all day. If you can't be there to add the milk, you can substitute evaporated milk for whole milk in all-day cooking. To use fresh milk, shorten the cooking time, make a white sauce with it before adding it to the pot, or add it only during the last hour of cooking.

SPICES WILL TASTE DIFFERENTLY

Since there is little evaporation in crockery pot slow-cooking, you may finish up with considerably more gravy or liquid than usual—sometimes more than you started with! So, you may discover that you want to add more seasonings after cooking. Seasoning is a matter of individual taste, anyway, and I'm sure you will soon learn to add to, or subtract from, the amounts of seasonings listed in the recipes in this book.

REDUCE GRAVIES BY HIGH COOKING OR THICKEN THEM

Extra liquid or gravy may be reduced (cooked

off and thus thickened) by turning up the temperature setting to HIGH and cooking *uncovered* until the gravy is as you want it. Before beginning this process, it is a good idea to remove the meat and vegetables from the gravy and keep them warm on a hot platter or in another pot in your oven.

If you want to keep the volume of your gravy but thicken it, use *beurre manié*—butter or margarine mixed with an equal amount of flour and rolled into little balls. Drop a few at a time into gravy, cooking on HIGH, and let it bubble until it's as thick as you want it to be. Some culinary experts advise making a roux of flour and fat cooked together then added to the gravy and cooked on HIGH until as you like it, but if the flour and fat are not completely cooked together before adding to the gravy, your gravy will taste pasty.

Cornstarch, potato starch, arrowroot, and tapioca will also thicken gravies. Cornstarch tends to break down when gravy is reheated. All these other methods, unlike the uncovered cooking first recommended, thicken gravies without reducing the volume.

BE CAREFUL WITH FROZEN FOODS

Consult the manufacturer's handbook before using frozen foods in a crockery pot slow-cooker. As a rule, it's not a good idea to put ice cold foods into a cooker. You might break the liner with the sudden cold. However, there are some liners which can take the cold—even storing in the refrigerator—and you may have one of them. It is always possible to add partly thawed vegetables to soups, stews, and chowders without danger to the crockery liner, if you do it when the pot is already cooking. This will not usually increase the cooking time appreciably.

DON'T TOUCH THE POT ONCE IT'S COOKING!

Once you have put the ingredients into your pot, plugged it in, and set the temperature control, *leave it alone!* Go do something else. If you need reassurance, sniff the steam or peer through the clear lid—but don't remove the cover unless you have to add something near the end of cooking time.

Low heat and slow-cooking for a long time are what make this cooking process different and distinctive, keep the vitamins whole and simmer in the flavors. Keeping the steam inside helps cook the food from the top. If you remove the lid just once, it requires about 15 to 20 minutes to build up steam and temperature again. And you can lose important nutrients in the escaped steam.

Once in a while a recipe calls for stirring at a certain point, but that is figured into total cooking time.

Don't lift the lid when baking—especially during the first two hours. It will absolutely ruin a bread or cake.

HOW TO SPEED UP SLOW-COOKING

There are a couple of ways you can speed up crockery pot slow-cooking without damaging the results: Use the HIGH setting instead of the LOW (one hour on HIGH equals two on LOW); or put a layer of aluminum foil under the cover of the pot. This acts as a reflector and increases the temperature of the area below.

BAKING HINTS AND PRECAUTIONS

Check the manufacturer's instructions for your make and model of crockery pot slow-cooker before trying to bake in it. Some cookers cannot be used dry, but must always contain a small amount of water for steaming, which may eliminate any chance of baking bread in them. If you can bake in it, find out if the manufacturer sells any type of baking chamber to be used inside. Otherwise, you will have to experiment with gelatin molds (metal), coffee cans, vegetable cans, ovenproof casseroles, souffle dishes, and ring-shaped or plain round cake tins. The bundt cake pan produces a delightfully crusty cake or bread. Sometimes you can bake round loaves of bread right in the crockery pot without an extra pan by oiling the liner and shaping the loaf to fit. Check each recipe for use of vents for steam, or for instructions about adding layers of paper toweling to absorb excess steam. Don't expect to get a browned top on your bread loaves, but they *will* be done in the time specified.

SAFETY HINTS AND MAINTENANCE ADVICE

Be certain to put your cooker on an adequately wide, level, and sturdy surface from which it cannot easily be pushed or pulled off accidentally. This applies to storage location as well as when in use.

Don't let the cord dangle where it can be pulled on to topple the pot or tripped over; nor should you let the cord touch any hot surface.

Don't ever re-use an extension cord that heats up. Throw it away. It's not adequate to the electrical load.

Keep the attached cord rolled up close to the

cooker when not in use. Wrap it with a plastic tie or a rubber band. The ties you get with trash bags are ideal for this purpose.

Never pull on the appliance cord to remove the plug from the wall socket, or the control from the cooker (if detachable). Grasp the plug firmly and remove it from the electrical outlet. Then grasp the removable control firmly and detach it from the pot. This should be your unvarying procedure with every electrical appliance cord: Always plug the cord into the appliance first, then into the socket; remove it by unplugging from the socket, then from the appliance. Then you will never be left with a live electrical cord in your hand!

At our house, in the working kitchen which doubles as our testing center for new recipes, we have a special drawer for kitchen appliance cords. To prevent them from tangling and also to prevent wear and tear, we coil them into individual tubes. At first we used the paper center tubes from toilet tissue rolls, but whenever a plastic tube or a heavy cardboard mailing tube came our way we transferred a cord to it. We leave the ends dangling outside the roll, so it's easy to locate any special cord by its distinctive male or female end.

I'd like to lay claim to this brilliant idea for protecting and separating appliance cords, but the truth is that our son Benjie brought the first tube home from school, suitably decorated and without toilet tissue, as a Mother's Day gift!

POT WASHING PRECAUTIONS

Unless the manufacturer's handbook says it can be done, never immerse a crockery pot slow-cooker completely in water. If the heating coils are part

26

of the cooker, it should be placed in an empty sink and filled with hot soapy water as soon as possible after being emptied of food. This will loosen any bits of food which might be clinging to the sides. Also, do not use cleansers, steel wool scouring pads, or any other abrasives or abrasive cleaning compounds on the crockery surface. This might damage the glaze. This also applies to cookers with detachable and removable crockery elements.

Never scratch the inside of a crockery cooker in any way to remove food stains or food. A scratch can provide a place for food to stick next time. And an especially deep scratch will trap food particles so they can never be cleaned out—providing a breeding place for bacteria. Which is a very good reason, also, for never putting knives, forks, or any other kitchen utensil to soak in your soapy crockery pot slow-cooker.

Many manufacturers recommend Dip It (or another similar Teflon cleaner) for removing persistent stains and restoring the finish of the crockery liner. Three or four tablespoons of cleaner should be added to enough hot water to cover the stains, then set the cooker on HIGH and cook for two hours (or overnight on LOW), and when the time is up rinse the cooker thoroughly and dry it well.

Whether or not the liner is detachable, you must remember that it is stoneware—highly glazed and nonporous—so it will show water spots and streaks like a window or mirror unless all soap or detergent is completely washed and dried off.

Slight discoloration of the crockery liner inside the cooker can be eliminated by wiping with a small amount of vegetable oil. The sparkle will be completely restored.

The crockery pot liner—like all stoneware—is easily broken or chipped, so be careful not to hit it against faucets or counter tops. A sudden sharp blow will almost certainly break it.

And watch out for sudden temperature changes. Don't wash a ceramic pot right after cooking unless you pour hot water into it. Also, don't use your crockery pot slow-cooker as a storage container in the refrigerator or freezer and don't put frozen or very cold food inside for cooking unless the pot has been preheated. This caution does not apply to detachable crockery pot liners, which may be used in the refrigerator for storage.

HANDLING SLOW-COOKERS WITH OTHER LININGS

Slow-cookers may be lined with, or made of, such other materials as glass, Corning Ware, porcelain, baked enamel, aluminum, stainless steel, and Teflon I or II. Because kind friends have loaned us other cookers, we have been able to learn the following special handling methods.

Wash stainless steel in hot soapy water, using a sponge or vegetable brush and cleanser. Use a steel wool scouring pad on the inside if you like, but never on the outside, because you'll never be able to polish away the scratches. Wash the outside with a sponge, cloth, or nylon scouring pad. Dry the pot completely and carefully or it will show water spots.

Pots made of combinations of metal—like Farberware Pot Pourri pans—may be cleaned with steel wool pads on the aluminum base, but never on the stainless steel.

Aluminum pots should be washed in hot soapy water, soaking off stubborn food stains or scrubbing them off with nylon or other plastic scouring pads. Use steel wool pads only if food is baked on very hard. To clean discolored aluminum, use Dip It or some other stain remover and wear gloves. Follow manufacturer's instructions for use of the stain remover—and don't get any of it on the outside of the cooker.

Porcelain and baked enamel liners should be completely cooled off before washing with hot soapy water, a dishcloth, sponge, or nylon pad. You may use a gently nonabrasive cleanser on porcelain (like Bon Ami), but never a metal pad or abrasive powder. Rinse and dry thoroughly.

Corning Ware is a ceramic glass material that will withstand tremendous temperatures and sudden temperature changes, so it can go right from the refrigerator to the heating unit. It usually cleans up easily with hot soapy water and a dish cloth or nylon scouring pad (metal pads scratch the glaze). Burned-on food will respond to baking soda or a nonabrasive cleanser and a damp cloth. Sugary or starchy burned-on foods should be soaked off or boiled off with a solution of 3 tablespoons of baking soda to a quart of water. If you use more water or a larger pot, increase the baking soda proportionately. Greasy foods should be cleaned off with a solution of ammonia and water.

Teflon should be washed with hot soapy water and thoroughly dried. Use a plastic scouring pad, but never a steel wool pad or an abrasive cleanser. They'll damage the coating. If you wash thoroughly after every use, you'll reduce the rate of normal discoloration over the heating element (which does not affect Teflon's resistance to sticking). However, if you don't like the stain, use Dip It or some other cleaner, following manufacturer's instructions and wearing gloves.

Never scrape or scratch any non-stick or Teflon surfaces, nor should you leave silverware or kitchen utensils soaking in pots with such surfaces. Like crockery, scratches can cause foods to stick and provide breeding spots for bacteria.

WATCH HOW YOU HANDLE HOT HANDLES AND OTHER SURFACES

Slow-cookers should be sufficiently well insulated as to be only moderately warm on their outside surfaces. But some of the metal-sided cookers with the coils encircling the inside to heat the liner are not that well protected. I shudder to think what could happen were someone to pick up a hot metal-sided slow-cooker, heavy with food, without adequate protection for hands and forearms. If your cooker heats up, be sure to wear heatproof padded gauntlets or use very large hotpads when handling it. We carefully inspected and discussed many different makes of cookers before we made our choice—paying particular attention to the position of handles, some of which were so low and small as to endanger the inner forearms, hands and, perhaps, the lower stomach by exposure to hot metal.

Be choosy about tops, too. Some are metal, some plastic or glass. All may heat up to some extent and burn fingers. Glass can also break. We chose a cooker with a clear plastic top which when not steamed up can be seen through, so you know there's something going on inside. It has a vent that comes in handy when baking. And it has a fairly heatproof plastic handle (Bakelite, I think), which won't break easily.

I realize this is a fairly forbidding compendium of instructions and cautions, but they *will* make it easier to use your crockery pot slow-cooker—and with more satisfying results.

HOW TO USE THESE RECIPES

There are four different categories of recipes in this book. Each recipe has a number following its title to indicate its category. Like this:

(1) A long-cooking recipe that will give you from 5 to 12 hours in which to do other things without watching your cooker.

(2) A shorter-time cooking recipe that is delicious when prepared in a crockery pot slow-cooker but only takes 2 to 4 hours to cook.

(3) Recipes for leftovers—for recycling foods from category 1 into new dishes.

(4) Recipes for things to go with crockery pot-cooked dishes. They are not cooked in the slow-cooker, but they certainly enhance the main dish—like salads, sauces, desserts, etc.

You can easily tell by the number after the title whether the recipe fits into your time pattern. After all, there are times, like weekends, when you have no need for long-cooking dishes.

HOW TO INCREASE COOKING TIMES

You can prepare recipes that only take a short time to cook, and still be away all day. Get an appliance timer. I use the same timer that turns our house lights on and off when we are away on vacation, or turns them on at night when we are going to be out after dark.

It has settings for all hours, and I plug it into a wall socket and then plug the slow-cooker into it. I set it to start at a time later in the day, but sufficiently early so that dinner will be ready when we return to eat it.

There are some timers with long cords (for

cookers with short cords) and other timers that can turn themselves off and on several times during a given period. Also, some kitchen ranges have timed receptacles that can double as timers when you plug appliances into them. The cost of an adequate appliance timer can range upwards from $5.95. There are deluxe timers which cost as much as $25. So, you're sure to find one to fit your pocketbook.

Well, that's all the preliminary advice I can give you. Now go, cook something good!

CHAPTER TWO
SOUPS

Beef Stock (Soup) (1)

Serves 6 to 8

1½ lbs. beef shank or
lean stewing beef,
cubed

8 cups water

1 leek (or a small
onion)

1 onion, quartered

3 cloves

2 ribs celery with
leaves

1 carrot, sliced

1 bay leaf

4 peppercorns

2 teaspoons salt

¼ teaspoon dried thyme
(optional)

Put the beef, water, leek, onion, cloves, celery, carrot, bay leaf, peppercorns, salt and thyme in your crockery pot slow-cooker. Cover and cook on LOW for 8 to 9 hours (or 4 to 5 hours on HIGH). Strain the broth and separate the meat from the vegetables. Discard the vegetables and serve the clear broth with chunks of meat in it as a soup (adding noodles, rice, or some other pasta—or dumplings). Or use the meat for a meal and reserve the soup as stock for use in other recipes. It may be kept in the freezer.

Chicken Stock (Soup) (1)

Serves 6 to 8

2½ lbs. chicken backs
and wings (or 1
chicken, cut-up)

1 leek (or 1 medium
onion)

1 onion, quartered

3 cloves

1 carrot, sliced

3 ribs celery with
leaves

1 bay leaf

4 whole peppercorns

2 teaspoons salt

¼ teaspoon dried thyme
(optional)

6 cups water

Wash and dry the chicken parts. Put them into your crockery pot slow-cooker, together with the leek, onion, cloves, carrot, celery, bay leaf, peppercorns, salt, thyme and water. (You may also add parsnip, parsley, dillweed, and such other vegetables as you prefer in your chicken soup—that is, if you are going to serve it as a soup. You may wish to keep the stock on the bland side until used in other soups, sauces, gravies, etc.) Cover the pot and cook this stock on LOW for 6 to 8 hours (or 3 to 4 hours on HIGH, if you're pressed for time). Strain the broth and discard the vegetables. Save the chicken meat and serve it in the soup. Or use the meat for a salad and reserve the stock for use in other recipes. It may be kept in the freezer.

Fish Stock (1)

Makes 2 quarts

2½ lbs. fish bones, heads, and other fish trimmings
8 cups water
2 teaspoons salt
10 peppercorns
1 rib celery, sliced
1 medium onion, chopped
1 tablespoon lemon juice
12 sprigs fresh parsley (or 2 tablespoons dried)
2 cloves
1 bay leaf
¼ teaspoon thyme
½ cup dry white wine

Combine fish bones and trimmings, water, salt, peppercorns, celery, onion, lemon juice, parsley, cloves, bay leaf, thyme and wine in your crockery pot slow-cooker. Cover and cook on LOW setting for 6 to 8 hours. Strain off the broth for use as stock in soups, gravies, for poaching fish, etc. This stock may be stored in the freezer.

Fish Chowder (1)

Serves 4 to 6

¼ lb. salt pork or
    bacon, diced
2 leeks (optional)
1 medium onion,
    chopped
1 rib celery, chopped
4 potatoes, peeled and
    diced

1 teaspoon salt
¼ teaspoon pepper
2 cups fish stock (or
    water)
2 cups evaporated milk
2 lbs. fish, fresh or
    frozen (red snapper,
    cod, halibut, etc.)

In a skillet, lightly fry the salt pork or bacon.
Remove the meat from the pan and reserve. Pour
off all but approximately 2 tablespoons of the
fat from the skillet and sauté the leeks, onion
and celery. Put the meat, leeks, onion, celery,
potatoes, salt, pepper, fish stock and evaporated
milk in your crockery pot slow-cooker. Cover and
cook on LOW setting for 6 to 8 hours. Add the
fish to the crockery pot and cook on HIGH for 1
to 2 hours more.

Cream of Fish Soup (2)

Serves 4

1 to 1½ lbs. firm
    white meat fish
1 medium onion,
    chopped
1 sprig fresh parsley
    (or ½ teaspoon
    dried parsley)
1 bay leaf

3 cups water (or fish
    stock)
1 tablespoon tomato
    puree
⅔ cup dry white wine
1 teaspoon salt
¼ teaspoon pepper

Fillet the fish, remove the bones, and cut it
into 2-inch pieces. Put the fish into your crockery
pot slow-cooker, together with the onion, parsley,
bay leaf and water. Cover the pot and cook on
LOW for 3 to 4 hours. Remove the fish pieces

from the liquid and set aside a few of the firmest pieces for garnish. Puree the rest of the fish in a blender, or mash it through a sieve and return it to the liquid in the pot. Add the tomato puree, wine, salt and pepper. Mix gently. Change the temperature setting to HIGH and heat until the soup simmers. Meanwhile, fry the fish pieces to a light brown and add them to the soup. Serve hot.

Sopa de Cuarto de Hora (2)

Serves 4 to 6

½ lb. uncooked shrimp
6 cups fish stock
   (see index)
4 oz. lean ham, diced
¼ cup sherry
   (optional)

Salt and cayenne pepper
   to taste
3 hardcooked eggs,
   chopped coarsely
1 cup cooked long
   grain rice

Peel and devein the shrimp. Combine shrimp, fish stock, ham, sherry, salt and cayenne pepper to taste, eggs, and the pre-cooked long grain rice in your crockery pot slow-cooker. Cover and cook on HIGH for 2 to 3 hours.

The name of this soup translates to "15 Minute Soup," but it takes a little longer in a crockery pot. Of course, the Spanish (and we) do not add in the 6 to 8 hours it takes to make the fish stock. What we actually have here is a supplement to a long cooking recipe—and a delicious way to put together a quick kind of *paella*.

Pot Au Feu (1)

Serves 4 to 6

1½ to 2 lbs. beef, round, shoulder or rump
8 cups water or beef stock
½ lb. beef bones
1 bouquet garni (parsley, thyme and bay leaf in cheese-cloth bag)
2 carrots, diced
2 turnips, diced
2 leeks, diced
½ clove garlic
1 medium onion
2 cloves
6 peppercorns
2 teaspoons salt
1 small cabbage, quartered

Put beef, water, bones and bouquet garni in your crockery pot slow-cooker. Add carrots, turnips, leeks and garlic. Cut onion in half and stick clove in each half. Add the onion halves and the salt. Cover the cooker and cook on LOW setting for 6 to 8 hours, or until the meat is tender. Add the cabbage quarters and cook on HIGH for 1 hour, or until the cabbage is done. Serve the vegetables in the soup and the sliced meat and cabbage as a second course. Complete the meal with French bread and a salad.

Meal-in-One Vegetable Soup (1)

Serves 6 to 8

1 lb. chuck bones (from chuck roast)
1 lb. beef shank bones
1 lb. beef chuck flat ribs
5 cups water
1 can (1 lb., 5 oz.) whole tomatoes
2 teaspoons salt
6 peppercorns
5 teaspoons beef bouillon crystals (or 5 cubes)
1 large carrot, sliced
3 ribs celery, sliced
1 large onion, diced

Combine bones, water, tomatoes, salt, pepper-corns, bouillon crystals (or cubes), carrot, celery and onion in your crockery pot slow-cooker and cook for 7 to 8 hours on LOW setting. Other vegetables may be added if desired.

This rich, full-bodied soup can be an entire meal, even for people with hearty appetites. A light dessert and beverage will complement it perfectly.

Scotch Broth (1)

Serves 4

1 lb. stewing beef, cubed
2 oz. dried split peas
1 carrot, diced
1 turnip, diced
2 leeks (or 2 small onions), quartered
2 to 3 oz. barley (raw)
2 teaspoons salt
1/4 teaspoon pepper
5 cups water

In your crockery pot slow-cooker, combine the beef, peas, carrot, turnip, leeks (or onions), barley, salt, pepper and water. Cover and cook on LOW setting for 8 to 10 hours.

Oxtail Soup from Germany (1)

Serves 6 to 8

2 large onions, chopped
2 large carrots, chopped
1 small piece of celeriac (celery root), chopped
2 lbs. oxtails, cut in 2-in. pieces
4 oz. lean ham or bacon, chopped
1 tablespoon butter or margarine
8 cups beef stock (or water)
1 teaspoon salt
1/4 teaspoon sugar
1/8 teaspoon red pepper (cayenne)
1 tablespoon flour
2/3 cup Burgundy or Madeira wine

Sauté the onions, carrots, celeriac, oxtails and ham (or bacon) in the butter (or margarine) un-

40

til lightly browned. Transfer to the crockery pot slow-cooker and add the stock (or water), salt, sugar and red pepper. Cover and cook on LOW for 8 to 10 hours, or until the meat is tender. Strain off the meat and vegetables. Return the liquid to the pot. Mix the flour with a little milk or water to make a thin paste. Stir this paste into the soup. Increase temperature to HIGH, bring the soup to a boil and stir constantly until the soup thickens. Remove the meat from the bones and add it to the soup, diced. When heated through, add the wine and serve hot.

Leek and Polish Sausage Soup (2)

Serves 4 to 6

¼ cup diced carrots
¼ cup diced celery
3 leeks, cut into ½-in. pieces
1½ cups diced potatoes
¼ lb. *kielbasa* (Polish sausage) or knockwurst, sliced thin
1 teaspoon salt

½ teaspoon marjoram
¼ teaspoon chervil
⅛ teaspoon pepper
3 cups chicken stock (see index) or bouillon
2 tablespoons flour
2 tablespoons butter or margarine

In your crockery pot slow-cooker, combine the carrots, celery, leeks, potatoes, sausage slices, salt, marjoram, chervil, pepper and chicken stock. Cover and cook on LOW for 5 hours. To thicken, remove ¼ cup of the liquid and combine it with the flour and butter, mixing well. Then return this mixture to the cooker and stir it well into the soup. Heat through and serve hot.

Pea Soup (1)

Serves 6

2 cups dried split peas	¼ lb. salt pork (or 1
1 cup chopped onion	ham hock)
½ cup sliced celery	1 teaspoon salt
1 bay leaf	6 peppercorns

Soak peas in water overnight. Drain. In your crockery pot slow-cooker, combine the peas with the onion, celery, bay leaf, salt pork, salt, peppercorns and enough water to cover. Cook on LOW for 10 to 12 hours. Discard the bay leaf. If the soup is too thick, thin it with hot milk.

Ham and Split Pea Soup (1)

Serves 6 to 8

3 lbs. smoked ham shank	2 cloves garlic, crushed
1½ cups green split peas	1 teaspoon salt
6 cups water	15 peppercorns (in a
¾ cup chopped celery	tea ball or cheese-
½ cup chopped carrots	cloth bag)
2 medium onions, chopped	Rind of 1 orange, grated
	2 knockwurst, sliced

Trim the fat and rind from the ham shank and put it into your crockery pot slow-cooker, along with the peas, water, celery, carrots, onions, garlic, salt, peppercorns and orange rind. Cover and cook on LOW for 8 to 10 hours. Remove the ham shank from the soup and cut the meat into bite-size cubes. Discard the bone and the peppercorns. Puree the soup and vegetables and return it to the crockery pot along with the cubes of ham. Re-set the control to HIGH, add the sliced knockwurst, cover, and cook for 30 minutes more.

Lamb Shank and Lima Bean Soup (1)

Serves 6 to 8

1 lb. lima beans
2 tablespoons fat or
other shortening
1½ lbs. lamb shanks
2 small onions, diced
2 carrots, diced
2 ribs celery, diced

1 clove garlic,
minced
1½ teaspoons salt
3 cups chicken stock
(or bouillon)
3 cups water

Soak the beans overnight in water to cover well, then drain. Heat the fat in a skillet and brown the lamb shanks all over. Put into your crockery pot slow-cooker the onions, carrots, celery, garlic, salt, beans, lamb shanks, stock and water. Cover and cook on LOW for 10 hours, or until the lamb is tender and the vegetables are done. Remove the lamb shanks, discard the bones and fat, and return the meat to the soup. Heat through and serve hot.

Lima Bean Soup (1)

Serves 6

1 cup small lima beans
½ cup pearl barley
1 onion, chopped
4 carrots, diced
6 ribs celery, chopped
½ small cabbage,
shredded fine
1 medium potato, diced

½ lb. spinach, in small
pieces
1 small package dried
mushrooms
¼ lb. butter or
margarine
1½ teaspoons salt
¼ teaspoon pepper
2 bouillon cubes

In your crockery pot slow-cooker, combine the beans, barley, onion, carrots, celery, cabbage, potato, spinach, mushrooms, butter, salt, pepper and bouillon cubes. Add enough water to cover. Cover the pot and cook on LOW for 8 to 10 hours.

Navy Bean Soup (1)

Serves 8 to 10

2 cups navy beans
1 cup chopped onion
3 sprigs of celery
leaves
1 bay leaf

1 smoked pork butt
(or 1 lb. ham in
chunks)
1 teaspoon salt
6 peppercorns

Soak the navy beans in water overnight. Drain
the beans. Put them into your crockery pot slow-
cooker, together with the onion, celery leaves,
bay leaf, pork, salt and peppercorns. Add water
to cover. Cook on LOW for 10 to 12 hours. Discard
the bay leaf and serve hot.

Black Bean Soup (1)

Serves 6

1 cup black beans
1 rib celery, chopped
1 medium onion,
chopped
1 leek, sliced
1 lb. smoked pork butt
(or picnic)
2 tablespoons chopped
parsley flakes

1 bay leaf
1 teaspoon pepper
1 qt. water
½ cup Madeira or
sherry wine
½ lemon, sliced thin
1 hardcooked egg,
grated

Wash the beans and soak them overnight in
enough water to cover. Combine the beans, celery,
onion, leek, meat, parsley, bay leaf, pepper and
water in your crockery pot slow-cooker. Cook on
HIGH for 3 hours, then lower temperature to
LOW and cook for 9 to 10 hours. Remove the
bay leaf and discard it. Remove the meat, discard-
ing fat and any bone, and cut it into small pieces.
Puree the beans and soup in your blender or food
mill. Return meat, beans and liquid to the crockery
pot. Raise the temperature to HIGH, add the

wine, cover and reheat the soup. When ready to
serve, ladle the soup into individual bowls, float
a slice of the lemon on top of each bowl, and
sprinkle the lemon slices with grated egg.

Hungarian Bean Soup (1)

Serves 4 to 6

½ lb. beans (red,
  brown, or white)
½ lb. smoked ham or
  pork, diced
1 large onion, diced
½ tablespoon paprika

1 clove garlic, diced
  fine
1 teaspoon salt
7 cups water
3 tablespoons chicken
  or goose fat (or lard)

Soak the beans in water to cover until they are
soft. This may take some time. Add them to your
crockery pot slow-cooker, together with the
smoked meat, onion, paprika, garlic, salt, water
and fat. Cover and cook on LOW for 12 to 24
hours. If a thicker soup is wanted, melt 1½
tablespoons of butter or margarine in a skillet
and stir in 1½ tablespoons of flour, stirring and
cooking until the mixture is smooth and bubbling.
Turn the heat control to HIGH, remove the cover
from the cooker, and stir in the flour-butter roux.
Continue to cook uncovered until the soup is as
thick as you like it.

In Hungary, this soup is eaten for breakfast,
or as a cure for hangovers, but it is also a delicious main dish, requiring only a light dessert to
make the meal complete.

Garbure [Basque-French Bean Soup] (1)

Serves 6 to 8

2 cups baby lima beans
Water
1 cup carrots, diced
1 cup turnips, diced
2 cups onions, diced
1 medium cabbage, shredded
8 small potatoes, peeled and quartered
1 cup fresh peas
2 lbs. salt pork or slab bacon
1 tablespoon dried parsley
1 small clove garlic (optional)
½ teaspoon thyme (optional)

Soak the beans overnight. Drain off water and add enough fresh water to make 8 cups. Put beans, water, carrots, turnips, onions, cabbage, potatoes, peas, meat, parsley and, if you wish, the garlic and thyme, into your crockery pot slow-cooker. Cover and cook on LOW for 8 to 10 hours, or until the meat is tender and the soup is "so thick that a soup ladle could stand up in it." Slice the meat and serve it as a separate course, after the soup.

This is an adaptation for the slow-cooker of a centuries-old recipe of which nobody knows the exact origin, Spanish or French. *Garbure* comes from the Spanish and means about the same as the French *ragôut*. It's popular in the Pyrenees, and also in the Béarn district of France. Wherever it came from, it's a good way to eat beans and vegetables.

Lentil Soup (1)

Serves 4 to 6

¾ lb. lentils, washed
2 carrots, coarsely
   chopped
1 large onion, chopped
½ cup celery leaves (or
   1 rib celery), chopped
1 bay leaf

1 large clove garlic,
   chopped
1 small hambone
5 cups beef broth (or
   water)
1 teaspoon salt
¼ teaspoon pepper
1 cup light cream

Into your crockery pot slow-cooker, put the lentils, carrots, onions, celery leaves (or chopped celery), bay leaf, garlic, hambone, broth (or water), salt and pepper. Cover and cook on LOW for 9 to 10 hours, or until the lentils are tender. Remove the hambone and skim off any fat. If there is meat on the hambone, cut it off and return it to the soup. Add the cream and cook on HIGH for 15 or 20 minutes, until thoroughly warmed. Serve with sliced frankfurters, diced ham, or grated cheese. In Iran, they mix 1 tablespoon of dried mint with ¼ teaspoon of ground pepper and ¼ teaspoon of ground cinnamon—and sprinkle it over the lentil soup just before serving.

Onion Soup (1)

Serves 6 to 8

3 onions, sliced in thin
   rings
¼ cup butter or
   margarine
1 teaspoon salt
1 tablespoon sugar
2 tablespoons flour

4 cups beef stock (see
   index) or bouillon
½ cup dry vermouth
   (or dry white wine)
French bread
Grated Parmesan cheese

Sauté the onion rings in the butter until they are soft, then add the salt and sugar, and cook for another 15 minutes. Stir in the flour and cook for 3 more minutes. Transfer the cooked onion rings to your crockery pot slow-cooker and add the stock and vermouth. Cover the pot and cook on LOW for 6 to 8 hours. Cut generous slices of French bread and toast them on both sides. Sprinkle each slice well on one side with grated Parmesan cheese and put them under the broiler flame until the cheese melts. Serve the soup in individual bowls with the cheese-bread slices floating on top of each bowl.

Celery Consomme (1)

Serves 4 to 6

1 large stalk celery, coarsely chopped	6 cups beef or chicken stock
Salt & pepper to taste	Croutons for garnish

Combine the celery, salt, pepper and stock in your crockery pot slow-cooker. Cover and cook on LOW for 6 to 8 hours (or on HIGH for 3 to 4 hours). Garnish with croutons and serve hot.

Corn Chowder (1)

Serves 4 to 6

2 oz. salt pork, diced	2 cups whole kernel corn
1 medium onion, chopped	2½ cups chicken stock
1 leek, chopped	1 teaspoon salt
1 rib celery, chopped	⅛ teaspoon pepper
2 potatoes, diced fine	Parsley for garnish
	Butter or margarine

Fry the diced salt pork in a skillet until the cracklings are crisp. Reserve the cracklings. Drain off all but 2 tablespoons of fat. Sauté the onion, leek and celery in the fat until light brown.

Transfer this mixture to your crockery pot slow-cooker. Add the potatoes, corn and stock. Add salt and pepper. Cover and cook on LOW for 6 to 8 hours. Change temperature setting to HIGH, add the milk, cover and cook for 1 more hour. Add some cracklings and chopped parsley to each serving bowl, together with a dab of butter. Serve hot.

Cream of Celery Soup (1)

Serves 4 to 6

1 whole stalk of celery (with leaves), chopped
1 small onion, chopped
1 large carrot, chopped
4 tablespoons butter or margarine
5 cups chicken stock
½ teaspoon salt
⅛ teaspoon white pepper
1 small bay leaf (optional)
⅛ teaspoon dried thyme (optional)
2½ cups milk
Nutmeg or parsley
Croutons

Sauté the celery, onion and carrot in the butter for about 10 minutes. Add them to your crockery pot slow-cooker, together with the stock, salt, pepper, bay leaf and thyme. Cover and cook on LOW setting for 6 to 8 hours, or until the vegetables are tender. Put the soup through a blender or sieve to puree it. Return the soup to the pot and set the temperature on HIGH. Stir in the milk. Cover and cook for ½ hour more. Add either nutmeg or parsley, and serve with croutons.

Minestrone (1)

Serves 6

¼ lb. minced salt pork (or ham)
1 can (16 oz.) chickpeas (garbanzos)
½ cup minced onion
1 clove minced garlic
½ cup diced carrots
1 cup fresh spinach, chopped
1 can (10 oz.) tomatoes, drained
½ cup diced celery
1 medium potato, diced
2 tablespoons chopped parsley
1 qt. chicken stock (or bouillon)
½ cup elbow macaroni (uncooked)
Grated Parmesan cheese

Sauté the salt pork and drain off the fat. Put the pork, chickpeas, onion, garlic, carrots, spinach, tomatoes, celery, potato, parsley, stock and enough water to cover (if stock does not) into your crockery pot slow-cooker. Cook on HIGH for 1 hour. Reduce temperature to LOW and cook for 6 to 8 hours. Add the macaroni about ½ hour before you are ready to serve, and cook until tender. Serve the minestrone in individual bowls, sprinkled generously with the grated Parmesan cheese.

Russian Borsch (1)

Serves 6 to 8

1 lb. fresh beets, peeled and grated
½ lb. potatoes, peeled and quartered
1 lb. cabbage, coarsely shredded
2 carrots, diced
2 onions, diced
1 small parsnip, diced (optional)
1 tablespoon tomato puree
2 tablespoons butter, margarine, or oil
1 tablespoon vinegar
2 teaspoons sugar
½ lb. hambone
1 tablespoon dried parsley
8 cups beef stock
Sour cream (or yogurt)

Into your crockery pot slow-cooker, put the beets, potatoes, cabbage, carrots, onions, parsnip, tomato puree, butter, vinegar, sugar, salt, hambone, parsley and stock. Cover and cook on LOW for 5 to 7 hours, or until the vegetables are tender. Serve with a dollop of sour cream in each bowl.

Beet Borsch with Orange Juice
(American Style) (1)

Serves 6

1 lb. beets	¾ teaspoon salt
4 cups clear beef stock	¼ teaspoon pepper
2 cups tomato juice	2 cups orange juice

Scrub and peel the beets. Grate them coarsely and add them to the beef stock, tomato juice, salt and pepper in your crockery pot slow-cooker. Cover and cook on LOW for 8 to 10 hours (or on HIGH for 4 to 5 hours). When ready to serve, add the orange juice to the borsch, set the pot on HIGH, and cook only until it bubbles. Serve hot or cold—with sour cream and chopped chives.

Creamed Borsch (1)

Serves 6

1 recipe Beet Borsch with Orange Juice (see preceding recipe)	2 egg yolks, beaten
	¾ cup cream (or evaporated milk)

Prepare the beet borsch with orange juice as in the preceding recipe, in your crockery pot slow-cooker. Puree the beets in a blender or through a fine sieve or food mill, then return the borsch to your pot. Combine the beaten egg yolks with the cream, then—using a plastic spoon—slowly combine this mixture with the borsch. Set

51

the slow-cooker on HIGH and heat through gently
—but do not boil. Garnish the borsch with
chopped chives and serve hot or cold.

Potage Dubarry
(Cauliflower Soup from France) (1)

Serves 6 to 8

1 large cauliflower
(or 2 small ones)
4 cups chicken stock
1 teaspoon salt

⅛ teaspoon white
pepper
1 cup cream
1 cup milk

Break the cauliflower into flowerets and combine them in your crockery pot slow-cooker with
the stock, salt and pepper. Cover and cook on
LOW for 6 to 8 hours. Put the stock through a
blender or sieve to puree it. Return the stock
to the pot, change temperature control to HIGH,
add the cream and milk and reheat. Do not boil.

Cream of Rabbit Soup (1)

Serves 6

1 rabbit, cut-up
1 lb. beef shank
1 large onion, chopped
1 bouquet garni
(parsley, thyme &
bay leaf in a cheese-
cloth bag)
1 carrot, chopped
1 rib celery, chopped
3 cloves
8 peppercorns

8 cups water
3 tablespoons butter
or margarine
3 tablespoons flour
½ cup port wine
(optional)
2 egg yolks
⅔ cup heavy cream (or
evaporated milk)
2 teaspoons salt

Wash and dry the rabbit parts and put them in
your crockery pot slow-cooker with the beef,
onion, bouquet garni, carrot, celery, cloves, peppercorns and water. Cover the pot and cook on

LOW for 6 to 8 hours, or until the meat is tender. Remove the rabbit and beef from the pot, discard all bones, and chop the meat very fine. Then put into a mortar or a blender and pulverize it. In a small saucepan, melt the butter and stir in the flour, cooking until it is well-mixed and bubbling. Remove the pan from the heat and stir in the pulverized meat. Add this mixture to the soup, change temperature to HIGH, cover the pot, and cook for 15 minutes. If you use port, add it here. Beat the yolks, stir them into the cream, then blend the mixture with the soup. Add the salt. Bring the soup to a simmer again, and serve.

CHAPTER THREE
BEEF, VEAL, PORK AND LAMB

Cholent (1)

Serves 6

1 cup dried lima beans	3 lbs. brisket of beef
1 cup raw barley	4 cups hot water
2 onions, diced	1½ teaspoons salt
1 clove garlic, minced	½ teaspoon pepper
3 tablespoons chicken fat or oil	1 teaspoon paprika
	¼ teaspoon ginger
	1 small bay leaf

Soak the lima beans overnight in water to cover. Drain the beans next morning and put them into your crockery pot slow-cooker, along with the raw barley. Sauté the onions and garlic in the fat or oil in a heavy skillet, then mix them with the beans and barley. Trim excess fat from the brisket and brown it on all sides in the skillet; then transfer the meat to the crockery pot, placing it on top of the beans and barley. Put 1 cup of water into the skillet, along with the salt, pepper, paprika and ginger. Stir and cook, scraping the bottom of the skillet to get the browned particles, until the ingredients are well blended. Pour this sauce into the crockery pot and add the rest of the water and the bay leaf. Cover and cook on LOW for 10 to 12 hours. The next recipe calls for the leftovers from this one.

Cholent Soup (3)

Serves 3 to 6

This isn't really a recipe, it's a family story. When we made the *Cholent* in our crockery pot slow-cooker, we decided to have it for dinner that night. But some of the family had other plans, so when we sat down to the table there were only 3 of us—a scant 3 when you consider that Benjie is seven years old, weighs 47 pounds, and is still wearing most of his size 6 slim clothes. He's not a feeding problem, he just doesn't have much capacity.

Well, we worked our way through the *Cholent* and the side dishes and sat for awhile around the table, contemplating our programs for the evening. Said Mary Lou, "What shall I do with the leftover *Cholent?* Nobody in the family cares for second-day food."

"Leave it to me," said I. "I'll think of something after I look into the pot." Which I did.

If you study the ingredients in the *Cholent,* it will soon come to you that the principle ones also fit into a bean-and-barley soup. I fished out the brisket and cubed it, returning it to the rest of the *Cholent* in the crockery pot. Then I added enough water to make a reasonably liquid soup, to which I contributed a couple of beef bouillon cubes for extra flavor, a handful (actually a tablespoon or so) of dried soup greens, and some sautéed mushrooms which were left over from something else. Then I covered the pot and let it cook on HIGH for about 3 hours. Cooled and packed into a large container in the refrigerator, this gave us material for lunches and dinners for several more days.

I wish I could be more definite about quantities, but when will you ever be left with the same amount of leftovers as I was anyway? Besides this is an exercise in creative cooking without a recipe. Try it.

Hoog-Shew Ngow-Naam
[Chinese Beef Plate Braised in Soy Sauce] (1)

Serves 4 to 6

2 lbs. beef plate
¼ cup rice wine or
   sherry
2 tablespoons sugar

8 to 10 slices fresh
   ginger root
½ cup soy sauce
Beef stock or hot water

Cut the beef plate into 1-inch cubes. Parboil them for 5 minutes, then drain well. Place the meat in your crockery pot slow-cooker, together with the wine, sugar, ginger, soy sauce and enough stock or water to barely cover the meat. Cover and cook on LOW for 8 to 10 hours, or until the beef is tender. Serve with hot, cooked rice. Note: Beef plate is a very inexpensive cut, which the Chinese call "white abdomen of beef" *(Ngow Bark Nahm)*, and is ideal for crockery pot slow-cooking.

Beef and Prunes (1)

Serves 6

1 pkg. (12 oz.) dried
   pitted prunes
2 cups Madeira (or
   other dry red wine)
2 lbs. boneless beef in
   1-in. cubes
4 tablespoons oil or fat
Salt and pepper to taste
3 onions, chopped
3 carrots, sliced

1 rib celery, chopped
2 bay leaves, flaked
1 teaspoon cinnamon
2 tablespoons sugar
2 tablespoons wine
   vinegar
3 medium potatoes,
   peeled and quartered
1½ tablespoons flour

Cook the prunes in the wine for 30 minutes, then drain them and set them aside, saving the wine for later use. Brown the beef cubes in the oil, adding salt and pepper to taste, then remove the meat from the skillet. In the pan juices, cook the onions, carrots and celery until they are translucent. Add the bay leaves, cinnamon and sugar. Combine the reserved wine with the vinegar. While stirring continuously, add the wine to the pan, cooking and stirring until the sauce is smooth. Put the potatoes and the beef cubes into your crockery pot slow-cooker and pour the sauce over them. Cover and cook on LOW for 5 to 7 hours, or until the meat is tender. Make a thin paste with the flour and some of the cooking sauce and then add it to the rest of the sauce in the pot. Add the reserved prunes, cover and cook on HIGH for another 30 minutes.

Roast Brisket of Beef (1)

Serves 6

6 carrots, cut in ½-in. rounds
6 medium potatoes, cut in half
3-4 lbs. brisket of beef

1 pkg. mushroom soup mix (or 1 pkg. onion soup mix)
¼ cup water

Put the carrots and potatoes in the bottom of your crockery pot slow-cooker. Trim the excess fat from the brisket and brown it in a heavy skillet on all sides. Place the meat on top of the vegetables and add the soup mix and water. Cover the crockery pot and cook on LOW for 8 to 10 hours, or until the meat and vegetables are tender.

Marinated Chuck Steak or Roast (1)

Serves 4 to 6

2 to 3 lbs. chuck steak or roast
⅓ cup wine vinegar
¼ cup ketchup
2 tablespoons soy sauce
1 teaspoon salt

2 teaspoons worcestershire sauce
1 teaspoon prepared mustard
¼ teaspoon garlic powder
¼ teaspoon pepper

Put the meat into your slow-cooking crockery pot. Combine the vinegar, ketchup, soy, salt, worcestershire, mustard, garlic powder and pepper and pour this mixture over the meat. Turn the steak or roast so it will be well-coated with the marinade on both sides. Cover the pot and cook on LOW for 6 to 8 hours, or until the meat is tender.

Chuck Steak with Peaches (1)

Serves 6

4 lbs. boneless chuck steak
Salt and pepper to taste
2 onions
1 can (12 oz.) peach nectar plus water to make 1 cup
Grated rind and juice of 1 lemon

1 teaspoon salt
¼ teaspoon pepper
½ teaspoon cinnamon
1 teaspoon ground cumin
1 tablespoon cornstarch
5 large ripe peaches, pitted

Season the steak to taste with the salt and pepper. Place it in your slow-cooking crockery pot. Using a blender or food grinder, puree the onions, nectar and water, lemon rind and juice, salt, pepper, cinnamon, cumin, cornstarch and 2 of the peaches. Pour this sauce over the meat, cover and cook on LOW for 6 to 8 hours, or until the meat is tender. Cut the remaining 3 peaches in halves and place them cut-side-down on the meat. Set the temperature control on HIGH, cover and cook for 20 to 30 minutes more.

Cuban Beef and Raisins (1)

Serves 6

3 lbs. beef chuck	6 tomatoes, peeled, seeded, and chopped coarsely
1½ teaspoons salt	
¼ teaspoon pepper	
4 tablespoons olive or salad oil	¼ teaspoon ground cloves
3 onions, chopped	1¼ teaspoons salt
2 cloves garlic, chopped	¼ teaspoon pepper
	¾ cup raisins
4 green peppers, chopped	3 tablespoons cider vinegar
1¼ teaspoons chili powder	⅓ cup pitted green olives, sliced (optional)
2 teaspoons sugar	

Trim the beef chuck and cut it into bite-size pieces. Put the meat into your crockery pot slow-cooker. Season with 1½ teaspoons of salt and ¼ teaspoon pepper. In a saucepan, heat the oil and cook the onions, garlic, peppers and chili powder until the vegetables are translucent. Add the sugar, tomatoes, cloves, salt and pepper. Cook until this mixture thickens slightly, then pour it over the beef in the crockery pot. Cover and cook on LOW for 5 to 7 hours, or until the meat is tender. Raise the temperature to HIGH and stir in the raisins, vinegar and olives. Cover and cook for 15 minutes more.

Basar Tz Aloouie
[Israeli Sweet-Sour Pot Roast] (1)

Serves 8 to 10

4 lbs. pot roast
3 cups onion, diced
1½ teaspoons salt
½ cup hot water
⅓ cup lemon juice

4 tablespoons brown
sugar
4 gingersnaps,
crushed

Brown the meat in a heavy skillet. Add the onions and brown lightly. Transfer meat and onions to your crockery pot slow-cooker and add salt, water, lemon juice, brown sugar and gingersnap crumbs. Cover and cook on LOW for 8 to 10 hours, or until the meat is tender. Serve with mashed potatoes, dumplings, or buttered noodles.

This recipe worked exceptionally well with the new "yearling beef" that has been appearing in the supermarkets, which appears to be range-fed young beef with no feedlot finishing. In fact, the labels on the packages advised "long slow cooking"—and what place is better than a crockery pot slow-cooker for that!

California Pot Roast (1)

Serves 8

3½-4 lbs. blade or arm
pot roast of beef
2 tablespoons flour
1½ teaspoons salt
⅛ teaspoon pepper
½ teaspoon curry
powder
3 tablespoons oil

¼ cup water
¼ cup honey
¼ cup soy sauce
2 tablespoons chopped
candied ginger (or
¼ teaspoon ground
ginger)
¼ cup flour

Trim off all fat from the meat. Combine the 2 tablespoons flour, the salt, pepper and curry powder and dredge the meat with this mixture.

Heat the oil in a heavy skillet or Dutch oven and brown the meat all over. Transfer the meat to your crockery pot slow-cooker. Combine the water, honey, soy sauce and ginger and pour the mixture over the meat. Cover the pot and cook on LOW for 6 to 8 hours, or until the meat is tender. Remove the meat from the pot and keep it warm. Increase the crockery pot temperature to HIGH. Add enough water to the liquid in the pot to make about 2 cups. Make a paste from a little of the hot liquid and the ¼ cup of flour. Gradually pour this paste into liquid in the pot, stirring constantly. Continue to heat to a smooth bubbling sauce. Slice the beef and arrange it on a platter. Pour the hot sauce over the meat on the platter and serve it right away.

Dinsztelt Marhahus
[Hungarian Pot Roast] (1)

Serves 8

4 lbs. pot roast (rump or brisket)	¾ cup tomato juice (or V-8 vegetable juice)
6 tablespoons cooking oil	1 cup beef stock or broth
½ teaspoon salt	2 cloves garlic, mashed
1 cup carrots (sliced ¼" thick)	12 peppercorns
1 cup onions (sliced ¼" thick)	1 bay leaf
2 tablespoons flour	⅛ teaspoon dried thyme

If you're using a brisket, trim off all excess fat. Brown the beef on all sides in 3 tablespoons of hot oil in a heavy skillet. Add salt. Put the browned meat into your crockery pot slow-cooker. Add the rest of the oil to the skillet, heat it, and cook the carrot and onion slices until the onion is translucent. Sprinkle on the flour and continue to cook and stir constantly until the flour is browned. Add the juice and stock to the skillet, simmer for 2 minutes, and stir—scraping up all browned meat particles. Add the garlic, peppercorns, thyme and bay leaf to the sauce and pour it over the meat. Cover the crockery cooker and cook on LOW for 8 to 10 hours, or until the meat is tender. Try serving this with potato dumplings, or egg noodles, or mashed potatoes.

Braised Beef Extraordinaire (1)

Serves 6

3 lbs. rump roast of beef
Bacon strips (or salt pork strips)
Nutmeg
¼ cup olive or salad oil
1 small onion, chopped fine
1 clove garlic, crushed
¼ teaspoon thyme
¼ teaspoon marjoram

2 teaspoons grated lemon peel
1 teaspoon salt
½ teaspoon pepper
4 tablespoons flour
4 tablespoons butter or margarine
10 small white onions
6 carrots, sliced thin
6 potatoes, quartered
½ cup beef stock (or boiling water)
½ cup red wine

Lard the roast with strips of bacon, then rub it with nutmeg. Combine the oil, onion, garlic, thyme, marjoram, lemon peel, salt and pepper, and rub this mixture over the meat. Dredge the meat with the flour and brown it all over in the butter, using a heavy skillet. Put the onions, carrots and potatoes in the bottom of your crockery pot slow-cooker and add the meat on top. Pour the stock and wine over the meat. Cover the pot and set the temperature control on LOW. Cook for 5 to 7 hours, or until the meat is tender.

Boeuf a la Mode [French Pot Roast] (1)

Serves 6 to 8

Traditionally, the meat would be marinated overnight in the refrigerator to heighten the flavors. Long cooking in the crockery pot slow-cooker makes this step unnecessary.

4 lbs. pot roast of beef	2 cloves garlic, minced
2 tablespoons olive oil (or salad oil)	3 tablespoons cognac (or domestic brandy, or 2 to 3 teaspoons brandy extract)
1½ cups dry red wine	
1 cup sliced onions	
2 bay leaves	12 small white onions
2½ teaspoons salt	4 carrots, diced
½ teaspoon pepper	12 mushroom caps (use stems in omelet)
¼ teaspoon thyme	
⅛ teaspoon mace	
2 tablespoons wine vinegar	1 veal knuckle

In a heavy skillet, brown the meat well on all sides. Set aside. Add the wine to the skillet, scraping the bottom to get up all of the browned meat particles. Place in your crockery pot slow-cooker the onions, bay leaves, salt, pepper, thyme, mace, vinegar, garlic, cognac, white onions, carrots and mushrooms. Add the browned meat and the veal knuckle, and pour the wine over all. Cover the pot and cook on LOW setting for 8 to 10 hours, or until the meat is tender. Serve on a hot platter, surrounded by the vegetables.

Beef Stew Deluxe (1)

Serves 6 to 8

2 lbs. beef chuck,
in 1½-in. cubes
¼ cup oil, butter, or
margarine
½ carrot, chopped fine
½ onion, chopped fine
1 tablespoon sugar
2 teaspoons salt
¼ teaspoon pepper
1 cup tomato juice
2 cups beef stock
(or hot water)
1 teaspoon
worcestershire sauce

1 bay leaf
1 clove garlic
½ cup chopped onion
(or 12 pearl onions)
6 medium carrots,
peeled and cut in
1-in. rounds
4 medium potatoes,
peeled and quartered
4 ribs celery, in 1-in.
lengths
2 cups prepared biscuit
mix (optional)

Brown the meat in hot oil in a heavy skillet. Remove the meat and pour off all but 2 tablespoons of the drippings. Sauté the chopped carrot and chopped onion in the fat, then add the sugar, stirring and cooking until the sugar is just carmelized a light brown. Combine the meat, carmelized mixture, salt, pepper, tomato juice, stock, worcestershire sauce, bay leaf, garlic, onion, carrots, potatoes and celery in your crockery pot slow-cooker, mixing well. Cover and cook on LOW for 8 to 10 hours. If dumplings are desired, make them according to the directions on the biscuit mix package and put them on top of this stew. Raise temperature to HIGH, cover, and cook for 30 minutes more.

Belgian Beef Stew (1)

Serves 4 to 6

2½ lbs. beef round, in 2-in. cubes
1 cup onion, chopped
2 tablespoons bacon fat (or oil)
1 teaspoon salt
½ teaspoon pepper
2 cups beer

1 tablespoon brown sugar
1 cup beef stock or broth
½ teaspoon crushed anise seeds (optional)
2 tablespoons flour

Sauté the beef and onion in the fat, in a heavy skillet. Transfer them to your crockery pot slow-cooker. In the skillet, using the pan drippings, combine the salt, pepper, beer, brown sugar and stock; then heat them just to the boiling point. Add this sauce to the crockery pot with the anise. Cover and cook on LOW for 6 to 8 hours, or until the meat is tender. Remove the meat and keep it warm. Make a thin paste of the flour and some of the sauce. Add this to the rest of the sauce in the crockery pot. Change setting to HIGH, cover and cook for 15 minutes more. Serve with hot noodles and, maybe, a salad of diced cucumbers, radishes and onions covered with sour cream.

Australian Braised Beef (1)

Serves 6 to 8

3 lbs. cross rib or beef rump, in ½-in. cubes
3 tablespoons butter or margarine
2½ cups beer
2 teaspoons salt
¼ teaspoon pepper
1 cup minced onion

⅓ cup grated carrot
1 tablespoon cornstarch
3 tablespoons orange juice
2 tablespoons grated orange rind
2 tablespoons currant jelly

Trim the fat from the meat. Melt the butter or margarine in a heavy skillet and brown the meat cubes. Transfer to the crockery pot slow-cooker. Combine the beer, salt, pepper, onion and carrot and pour over the meat. Cover and cook on LOW for 5 to 7 hours, or until the meat is tender. Mix the cornstarch with the orange juice and stir it into the gravy with the orange rind and the jelly. Increase the temperature to HIGH and cook for another 15 to 20 minutes, covered.

Boeuf a la Flamande [Flemish Beef Slices] (1)
Serves 8 to 10

2 tablespoons butter or margarine	1 cup diced carrots
4 lbs. rump or round of beef, in ½-in. slices	2 teaspoons salt
	½ teaspoon pepper
	2 cups beer
2 cups sliced onions	1 tablespoon sugar
	½ teaspoon thyme

Melt the butter in a heavy skillet and brown the beef strips all over. Put the carrots and onions in the bottom of your crockery pot slow-cooker. Add the browned meat, salt, pepper, beer and sugar. Cover the pot and cook on LOW for 4 to 6 hours. Raise the temperature to HIGH and add the thyme. Cover and cook for 20 to 30 minutes more.

Beef Stroganoff (1)
Serves 4 to 6

2 lbs. round steak, ½-in. thick	1 clove garlic, minced
3 tablespoons butter or margarine	1 teaspoon worcestershire sauce
½ cup minced onion	4 tablespoons tomato sauce
½ lb. sliced mushrooms	2 cups sour cream (or thick yogurt)
1¼ teaspoons salt	
¼ teaspoon pepper	

Cut the steak into strips 1½ inches by ¼ inch. Melt the butter in a heavy skillet and sauté the onions and mushrooms, then brown the meat. Transfer the contents of the skillet to your crockery pot slow-cooker and add salt, pepper, garlic, worcestershire sauce and the tomato sauce. Cover the crockery pot and cook on LOW for 6 to 8 hours, or until the meat is tender. Increase the temperature to HIGH and add the sour cream. Cover and cook for about 15 minutes, or until the sour cream is heated through, but not boiling. Serve over rice or noodles.

Deviled Short Ribs of Beef (1)

Serves 4 to 6

3 lbs. short ribs, in serving size pieces	2 tablespoons prepared mustard
2 teaspoons salt	¼ cup vegetable oil
½ teaspoon pepper	¼ cup chopped onion
1 teaspoon chili powder	1 clove garlic, minced
½ teaspoon sugar	¾ cup beef broth or bouillon
2 tablespoons lemon juice	1 tablespoon flour

Trim the fat from the meat and brown the pieces of short rib in a heavy skillet. Transfer the meat to your crockery pot slow-cooker. In a separate bowl, mix together the salt, pepper, chili powder, sugar, lemon juice, mustard, oil, onion, garlic and beef broth. Pour this mixture over the meat in the pot. Cover and cook on LOW for 5 to 7 hours, or until the meat is tender. Next, turn the temperature control to HIGH. Make a paste of the flour and some of the gravy and combine this paste with the liquid in the pot. Cover and heat until the gravy is bubbling and smooth.

Polish Short Ribs of Beef (1)

Serves 4 to 6

4 lbs. short ribs, cut in serving pieces
2 slices bacon, diced
1½ cups chopped onion
1½ teaspoons salt
2 tablespoons caraway seeds
⅓ cup wine vinegar
1 cup hot water

Trim the fat from the meat. Brown the bacon in a skillet, then add the onions and short ribs. Cook over medium heat for 10 minutes, stirring often. Transfer the contents of the skillet to your crockery pot slow-cooker. Add the salt, caraway seeds, vinegar and water, and mix well. Cover the pot and set the temperature control to LOW. Cook for 5 to 7 hours, or until the meat is tender. Skim off all fat before serving this dish.

Fresh Beef Tongue (1)

Serves 4 to 6

1 fresh beef tongue (3 lbs.)
1 bay leaf
6 peppercorns
6 cloves
1 medium onion
1 tablespoon salt
1½ cups water

Wash the tongue well. Put it into your crockery pot slow-cooker and add the bay leaf, peppercorns, cloves, onion, salt, and water. Cover and cook on LOW for 9 to 10 hours, or until the tongue is tender. Cool until the tongue can be handled, then peel off the outer skin and trim off the fat.

Glazed Beef Tongue (2)

Serves 4 to 6

1 cooked Beef Tongue,
   3 lbs. (see preceding
   recipe)
1½ cups dry white wine

¼ cup honey
1 teaspoon cinnamon
4 thin slices lemon

Slice the cooked tongue into ¼-inch slices and arrange them in the bottom of your slow-cooking crockery pot. Combine the wine, honey, cinnamon and lemon slices and pour this mixture over the meat. Cover the pot and cook on the HIGH setting for 2 to 3 hours.

Rolled Stuffed Flank Steak (1)

Serves 6

2 onions, chopped
1 teaspoon dried sage,
   crushed (or thyme)
2 tablespoons salad oil
1½ cups fine bread
   crumbs
1 teaspoon chopped
   parsley (or celery
   leaves)

¾ teaspoon salt
⅛ teaspoon pepper
2 to 3 lbs. flank steak
1 pkg. dry mushroom
   soup mix
2½ cups water
1 tablespoon flour
¼ cup water

In a heavy skillet, sauté the onions and sage in the salad oil. Combine the bread crumbs and the parsley, then mix them thoroughly with the ingredients in the skillet. Add the salt and pepper. Pound the flank steak thin with a mallet or heavy bottle. Spread the stuffing evenly over the meat, then roll the meat lengthwise and tie it or secure the roll with skewers. Rub the sides and bottom of your crockery pot slow-cooker with oil lightly, and carefully insert the rolled steak. Make the sauce by combining the soup mix with the 2½ cups of water in a medium saucepan and stirring until smooth, then heat it to the boiling point, stirring occasionally. Next, simmer the sauce for 3 minutes. Mix the flour with the remaining ¼ cup water and add it to the hot sauce, continuing to stir and cook until thick. Pour the sauce over the meat in the crockery pot and cook on LOW for 8 to 10 hours, or until tender.

Dutch Beef Birds with Onions (1)

Serves 6

1½ lbs. round steak
2 teaspoons salt
¼ teaspoon pepper
¼ teaspoon marjoram
6 small white onions
¼ cup flour

2 tablespoons vegetable oil
1 can (20 oz.) tomatoes
2 tablespoons prepared horseradish

Cut the meat in six slices and pound them thin. Season with salt, pepper and marjoram. Place an onion on each slice, roll up, and tie with thread or fasten with toothpicks. Roll these birds in the flour. Heat the oil in a heavy skillet and brown the rolls all over. Transfer them to your crockery pot slow-cooker. Add the tomatoes and horseradish. Cover and cook on LOW setting for 7 to 9 hours, or until the birds are tender.

Greek Moussaka (1)

Serves 6 to 8

2 medium eggplants
½ cup flour
½ cup olive or salad oil
1 large onion, chopped
1 clove garlic, chopped
¾ lb. ground lean beef
¾ lb. ground lean lamb
1 can (8 oz.) tomato sauce
½ teaspoon salt
¼ teaspoon pepper

½ teaspoon allspice
2 cups grated Parmesan cheese
1 cup dry bread crumbs
6 tablespoons butter or margarine
3 cups milk
3 eggs, well beaten
1 teaspoon salt
¼ teaspoon pepper

73

Slice off the stem ends and cut the eggplants crosswise into ½-inch slices. Sprinkle them well with salt and let them stand about 20 minutes. Wash off the salt and dry the eggplant slices with paper towels. Dip both sides of the slices into flour and fry them in hot oil, ½-inch deep, until lightly browned on both sides. Drain the slices on paper towels. Heat 2 tablespoons of oil in a skillet and sauté the chopped onion and garlic until the onion is a golden brown. Add the beef and the lamb and cook until all the red color is gone from the meat, breaking up the lumps with a fork while it cooks. Add the tomato sauce and simmer for 10 minutes. Season with ½ teaspoon salt, ¼ teaspoon pepper and the allspice. Lightly grease your crockery pot (or spray it well with lecithin) and place a layer of eggplant slices on the bottom. Spoon half of the meat sauce over this, then ½ cup of the grated cheese, and ⅓ cup of the bread crumbs. Top with a layer of eggplant slices and repeat this layering process. In a saucepan, melt the butter and stir in the flour, mixing well. Stir and cook until bubbly and smooth. Next, gradually stir in the milk and 1 cup of the grated cheese. Stirring constantly, continue to cook at low heat until the mixture bubbles and thickens. Stir this hot sauce slowly into the beaten eggs, then season with 1 teaspoon of salt and ¼ teaspoon of pepper. Spoon this sauce over the eggplant in the crockery pot slow-cooker and sprinkle it with the remaining bread crumbs. Cover and cook on LOW for 5 to 7 hours. Cut into squares to serve.

Stuffed Cabbage Rolls (1)

Serves 6 or more

12 large cabbage leaves
1 lb. ground beef (or lamb)
½ cup cooked rice
½ teaspoon salt
⅛ teaspoon pepper
¼ teaspoon thyme

¼ teaspoon cinnamon
½ onion, grated
½ apple, grated
½ cup brown sugar
2 tablespoons vinegar
Juice of ½ lemon
2 cups canned tomatoes

Wash the cabbage leaves. Bring 4 cups of water to a boil. Soak the leaves in the hot water (off the heat) for about 5 minutes, then remove them, drain and let cool. Combine the ground meat, cooked rice, salt, pepper, thyme, cinnamon, onion and apple. Place about 2 tablespoons of this mixture on each leaf near the center, fold up the bottom, fold in the sides, then roll up tightly. If you have extra cabbage leaves, put some on the bottom of the crockery pot slow-cooker. Then put the cabbage rolls in, seam side down. Add the brown sugar, vinegar, lemon juice and tomatoes. Cover and cook on LOW for 8 to 10 hours.

Ground Beef and Potato Casserole (1)

Serves 4 to 6

1 lb. ground beef
1 can (8 oz.) tomato sauce
1 can (12 oz.) Mexicorn kernels, drained
¼ cup minced onion
1 teaspoon salt

⅛ teaspoon pepper
1½ cups dry mashed potato flakes
1½ cups sour cream or yogurt
⅓ cup water
1½ cups grated sharp cheddar cheese

Brown the ground beef in a heavy skillet, stirring it with a fork to break up the lumps. Drain off all fat. Transfer the meat to your crockery pot slow-cooker and add the tomato sauce, corn, onion, salt and pepper. Mix thoroughly. In another bowl, combine the potato flakes with the sour cream and water. Spread this mixture over the beef. Top with the grated cheddar cheese. Cover and cook on LOW for 8 to 10 hours.

Meat Loaf (1)

Serves 4 to 6

1 medium onion, diced
1 tablespoon butter or margarine (or oil)
⅔ cup beef stock (or bouillon, or tomato juice)
1½ teaspoons salt
½ teaspoon pepper
1 teaspoon dried parsley (optional)

2 eggs
½ cup bread crumbs (or wheat germ)
2 lbs. lean ground beef
½ cup ketchup (or tomato sauce)
2 tablespoons brown sugar
½ teaspoon worcestershire sauce

Sauté the onion in the butter in a small skillet. In a large bowl, combine the stock, salt, pepper, parsley, eggs and bread crumbs. Mix well. Add the ground beef and combine thoroughly, using clean hands or a fork. Form into any desirable shape to fit the crockery pot slow-cooker (I prefer a round loaf). Set the loaf into the pot and cover it with a sauce made by combining the ketchup, brown sugar and worcestershire sauce. Cover and cook on LOW for 6 to 7 hours. Let stand for 10 minutes before slicing.

Sweet and Sour Meat Balls (2)

Serves 6

1 can (28 oz.) whole
  tomatoes
1 can (8 oz.) tomato
  sauce
2 tablespoons lemon
  juice
2 tablespoons brown
  sugar
6 gingersnaps, crushed
1 egg
1 onion, grated

¼ cup fine bread
  crumbs
¼ teaspoon garlic
  powder
1½ teaspoons salt
½ teaspoon pepper
2 tablespoons chopped
  parsley
2 lbs. lean ground beef
2 tablespoons fat or
  oil

In the crockery pot slow-cooker, combine the tomatoes, tomato sauce, lemon juice, sugar, and crushed gingersnaps. In a large bowl, mix together the egg, onion, bread crumbs, garlic powder, salt, pepper and parsley. Add to this mixture ½ cup of the sauce in the crockery pot; also add the ground beef. Mix well to blend all ingredients. Form small meat balls and brown them all over in a heavy skillet, using the 2 tablespoons of fat or oil. When browned, transfer the meat balls to your slow-cooker, cover, and cook on LOW for 4 to 6 hours. Serve with boiled little potatoes, or cooked hot rice.

Polpette Parmigiana [Meat Balls Parmesan] (2)

Serves 6 to 8

1½ lbs. ground beef
¾ cup grated Cheddar
  cheese
1 cup chopped
  cooked spinach,
  drained
1 clove garlic, minced
3 tablespoons minced
  parsley

¾ cup chopped onion
1½ teaspoons salt
½ teaspoon pepper
½ cup flour
½ cup salad oil
2 cans (8 oz. ea.)
  tomato sauce
⅓ cup grated Parmesan
  cheese

Combine the beef, Cheddar cheese, spinach, garlic, parsley, onion, salt and pepper. Chill this mixture for 30 minutes in the refrigerator. Shape the mixture into 2-inch balls. Roll them in the flour and brown them in the oil in a hot skillet. Transfer the meat balls to your crockery pot slow-cooker and add the tomato sauce. Cover and cook on LOW for 4 to 6 hours. Raise the temperature to HIGH and sprinkle the meat balls with the Parmesan cheese. Cover and cook for 15 more minutes.

Lihapyorykat
[Finnish Beef Balls in Dill Sauce] (2)
Serves 4 to 6

1 lb. ground beef
1½ cups grated raw potatoes
½ cup minced onion
½ cup chopped green peppers
1 tablespoon minced dillweed (or ½ tablespoon dill seed)
1½ teaspoons salt
½ teaspoon pepper
2 tablespoons oil
¾ cup canned tomato sauce
1 tablespoon worcestershire sauce
½ cup water
¼ cup chopped dill pickle

Combine the beef, potato, onion, green peppers, dill, salt and pepper. Shape into 1-inch balls. Heat the oil in a skillet and brown the meat balls all over. Transfer the browned meat balls to your crockery pot slow-cooker. Combine the tomato sauce, worcestershire sauce, water and pickles. Pour this mixture over the meat balls in the pot. Cover and cook on LOW for 4 to 6 hours. Serve with cooked noodles or rice.

Sformata di Carne e Riso
[Italian Rice-Beef Mold] (2)

Serves 4 to 6

1 lb. ground beef
1½ teaspoons salt
¾ teaspoon pepper
½ teaspoon oregano
2 egg yolks
¼ cup minced onion

½ cup peeled and
chopped tomatoes
4 cups cooked rice
3 tablespoons butter or
margarine
¼ cup grated Parmesan
cheese

Combine the ground beef, salt, ½ teaspoon of the pepper, the oregano, egg yolks, onion and tomatoes. Mix the rice with the remaining pepper and add additional salt if necessary. Butter a 6-cup mold or a 1½-quart round baking dish. Line the bottom and sides of the mold with 3 cups of the rice. Put the meat mixture in the center and spread the remaining rice on top. Dot with butter and sprinkle with grated cheese. Cover the mold with aluminum foil (tie it on with string if you think it won't stay in place). Place the mold on a trivet in your crockery pot slow-cooker and add 1 cup of hot water. Cover and cook on HIGH for 2 to 3 hours. Unmold onto a heated platter and serve with a spicy tomato sauce if you desire.

Polpettone alla Siciliana
[Sicilian Beef Roll] (1)

Serves 6 to 8

1½ lbs. ground beef
½ cup tomato juice
2 eggs, beaten
½ cup soft bread
crumbs
1½ teaspoons salt
½ teaspoon pepper
¼ teaspoon oregano

2 cloves garlic,
minced
3 tablespoons parsley,
minced
8 slices cooked ham
8 slices mozzarella
cheese

Combine the ground beef, tomato juice, eggs, bread crumbs, salt, pepper, oregano, garlic and parsley. On a large sheet of wax paper, pat out the mixture into a rectangle approximately 10 by 16 inches. Arrange the ham slices and cheese slices on this rectangle, then roll it up like a jellyroll, lifting the paper as you roll. Lightly grease the crockery pot slow-cooker or spray it inside with lecithin. Form the meat roll to fit the inside of the crockery pot, in a sort of semi-circle, lifting it carefully from the wax paper into the pot. Cover and cook on LOW for 6 to 8 hours. Let the meat roll stand at room temperature for 15 minutes before slicing and serving.

Manzo Ripieno [Italian Beef Rolls] (1)

Serves 4 to 6

2 lbs. flank steak, pounded thin
2 slices white bread
½ cup milk
¼ lb. chicken livers, diced
¾ cup chopped onion
¼ cup chopped celery
¼ cup minced parsley
¼ cup grated Parmesan cheese

¼ lb. cooked tongue, in julienne strips
1 egg, beaten
2½ teaspoons salt
¾ teaspoon pepper
¾ teaspoon oregano
3 tablespoons olive oil (or salad oil)
1½ cups beef stock (or broth)

Trim the fat from the meat. Soak the bread in the milk for 10 minutes, drain, and mash smooth. Combine the bread with the livers, onion, celery, parsley, cheese, tongue, egg, 1 teaspoon of the salt, ¼ teaspoon of the pepper and ¼ teaspoon of the oregano. Spread this stuffing mixture on the flank steak. Roll the steak up and secure it with string or toothpicks. Heat the oil in a heavy skillet and brown the roll on all sides.

Transfer the roll to your crockery pot slow-cooker and sprinkle it with the remaining salt, pepper and oregano. Cover and cook on LOW for 8 to 10 hours, or until the meat is tender. Let the roll stand at room temperature for 15 to 20 minutes before slicing.

Mexican Lima Bean-Beef Casserole (1)

Serves 6 to 8

2 tablespoons butter or margarine
1 large onion, chopped
1 clove garlic, minced
1 green pepper, chopped
1 lb. ground beef
2½ cups canned tomatoes
1½ teaspoons salt
½ teaspoon paprika
¼ teaspoon pepper
⅛ teaspoon cayenne pepper
1 tablespoon chili powder
2½ cups cooked lima beans (or 1 cup uncooked beans soaked overnight)

Melt the butter in a skillet and cook the onion, garlic and green pepper until the onion is golden. Add the ground beef and cook until lightly browned, stirring it with a fork to get all the meat cooked. Combine the sautéed vegetables and beef in your slow-cooking crockery pot with the tomatoes, salt, paprika, pepper, cayenne, chili powder and beans, mixing well. Cover and cook on LOW for 6 to 8 hours.

Leftover Beef Hash (1)

Serves 4 to 6

2 to 3 cups cooked beef, cut up fine
2 pkges. (10 oz. ea.) frozen hash brown potatoes, thawed
1 onion, diced
¼ cup melted butter or margarine (or oil)
1 cup beef stock or gravy (see index)
Salt and pepper to taste

In your crockery pot slow-cooker, combine the meat with the potatoes, onion, melted butter and stock. Add salt and pepper to taste. Cover and cook on LOW for 6 to 8 hours.

Beef Pot Pie (1)

Serves 4

2 lbs. chuck or round steak, in 1-in. cubes
3 tablespoons flour
1 teaspoon salt
⅛ teaspoon pepper
2 sliced carrots

1 sliced potato
1 onion, diced
2 cups canned tomatoes
1 pastry crust (see index)

Toss the beef cubes in a mixture of the flour, salt and pepper until thoroughly coated, then put them into your crockery pot slow-cooker. Add the carrots, potato, onion and tomatoes. If you want a brown gravy, add Brown-Quick, Kitchen Bouquet, Gravy Master, soy sauce, or some other browning agent, according to package directions. Cover and cook on LOW for 7 to 10 hours. About 1 hour before you intend to serve, transfer the contents of the crockery pot to a shallow 2½-quart baking dish. Cover with a pastry crust. Cut slits in the top to allow the steam to escape. Put into a preheated oven (425 degrees Fahrenheit), and bake for 20 to 25 minutes—until the top is well browned.

Steak and Kidney Pie (1)

Serves 4

1½ lbs. beef or veal kidneys
1½ lbs. round steak or chuck steak in 1-in. cubes
1 onion, diced

1 cup beef stock or bouillon
1 teaspoon salt
½ teaspoon pepper
1 pastry crust (see index)

Cook the kidneys in salt water for about 10 minutes, then let cool so you can handle them. Remove excess fat, tubes, and other tissues, then cut the kidneys into 1-inch cubes. Put the kidney pieces, steak cubes, and onion into your crockery pot slow-cooker. Add the stock, salt and pepper. If you want a brown gravy, add Brown-Quick, Gravy Master, Kitchen Bouquet, or another browning agent, according to package directions. Cover and cook on LOW for 8 to 10 hours. Preheat your oven to 400 degrees Fahrenheit, transfer the contents of your crockery pot to a baking dish and top it with a pastry crust. Cut slits to let the steam escape. Bake the pie for 15 to 20 minutes, or until the top is well browned.

Veal in Sour Cream (1)

Serves 4

1½-2 lbs. veal steak	1 clove minced garlic
¼ cup flour	2 cubes beef bouillon
1 teaspoon salt	1 cup hot water
1 tablespoon paprika	1 cup canned tomatoes
⅛ teaspoon pepper	½ cup sour cream (or
1 tablespoon parsley	yogurt)
flakes	3 tablespoons flour
1 onion, chopped fine	

Remove all fat and bone from the veal and cut it into 1½-inch cubes. Combine the ¼-cup flour with the salt, paprika, pepper and parsley flakes in a plastic bag and toss the meat cubes in it to coat them thoroughly. Transfer the coated meat to your crockery pot slow-cooker. Add the onion and garlic. Dissolve the bouillon cubes in the hot water and add the stock to the pot, together with the tomatoes. Stir well. Mix the sour cream with the 3 tablespoons of flour and add the mixture to

the pot, stirring everything together thoroughly.
Cover and cook on LOW for 8 to 10 hours.

Sloppy Joe Sandwiches (1)

Serves 6 to 8

2½ lbs. ground beef
1 onion, minced
1 cup ketchup
1 teaspoon chili powder
1 teaspoon dry mustard
2 cups beef stock or
  bouillon (see index)
Hamburger buns, toasted

Brown the ground beef in a heavy skillet,
separating all lumps with a fork. Drain well.
Transfer the meat to your crockery pot slow-
cooker and add the onion, ketchup, chili powder,
mustard, and stock. Mix well. Cover and cook on
LOW for 6 to 10 hours. Serve on toasted hamburger rolls.

Bo-Lo Pai Goot
[Chinese Spareribs with Pineapple] (1)

Serves 3 to 4

3 lbs. pork spareribs
1 cup soy sauce
1 cup pineapple juice
½ cup sugar
½ cup vinegar
½ cup water
3 tablespoons flour
2 cups pineapple
  chunks (drained)
2 tablespoons
  cornstarch

Trim excess fat from the spareribs and cut into
serving-size pieces. Marinate 2 to 3 hours in the
soy sauce, drain and put them on a rack in a shallow roasting pan. Roast the ribs, meaty side up,
for 30 minutes in a preheated 450 degree Fahrenheit oven. Transfer the ribs to your crockery pot
slow-cooker. Combine the flour with a little of
the pineapple juice, stir well and gradually add
the rest of the juice, the vinegar, sugar and

water. Pour this sauce over the spareribs, cover the crockery pot and cook on LOW for 6 to 8 hours. Raise the temperature to HIGH, add the pineapple chunks, dissolve the cornstarch in a little cold water and stir it into the pot. Cover and cook on HIGH for 10 to 15 minutes, or until the sauce is heated through and slightly thickened.

Chinese Baked Spareribs (1)
Serves 3 to 4

3 lbs. pork spareribs
1/4 cup prepared mustard
1/4 cup light molasses
1/4 cup soy sauce
3 tablespoons cider vinegar
2 tablespoons worcestershire sauce
2 teaspoons Tabasco sauce

Preheat the oven to 450 degrees. Cut the ribs into serving pieces and put them on a rack in a shallow baking pan. Roast the ribs, meaty side up for 30 minutes. Combine the mustard, molasses, soy sauce, vinegar, worcestershire and Tabasco sauces. Pour over the ribs in the crockery pot slow-cooker. Cover and cook on LOW for 6 to 8 hours.

Mexican-Style Barbecued Spareribs (1)
Serves 4

3 to 4 lbs. loin back ribs of pork
1 cup ketchup
1/3 cup worcestershire sauce
2 teaspoons chili powder
1 teaspoon salt
1/4 teaspoon Tabasco sauce
1 cup water

Preheat your oven to 450 degrees. Cut the ribs into serving-size portions. Place them on a rack in a shallow baking pan. Roast for 30 minutes, meaty side up. Transfer the ribs to your crockery pot slow-cooker. In a saucepan, combine the ketchup, worcestershire sauce, chili powder, salt, Tabasco sauce, and water. Bring this mixture to a boil and pour it over the ribs in the crockery pot. Cover and cook on LOW for 6 to 8 hours.

Stuffed Pork Chops (1)

Serves 4

4 double loin pork chops, cut 1½ inches thick
1 onion, chopped
1 tablespoon butter or margarine
½ cup soft bread crumbs

1 teaspoon salt
½ teaspoon pepper
⅛ teaspoon nutmeg
4 prunes, cooked, seeded, and chopped
Prune juice for basting
Juice of 1 lemon

Cut a pocket in each chop. Sauté the chopped onion in the butter in a heavy skillet. Stir in the crumbs, salt, pepper, nutmeg, prunes and a little prune juice if this mixture is too dry. Stuff the mixture into the pockets in the chops and secure with skewers or wooden toothpicks. Lightly grease your crockery pot slow-cooker and put the chops inside. Pour the lemon juice over the chops and baste with a little prune juice before covering. Cover and cook on LOW for 6 to 8 hours.

Polish-Style Pork Chops (1)

Serves 4

4 loin pork chops
3 tablespoons chopped onion
1 can (8 oz.) tomato sauce
1 dill pickle, chopped fine

¼ cup dry sherry
1 teaspoon salt
¼ teaspoon pepper
½ cup sour cream (or yogurt), at room temperature

Brown the chops well all over in a heavy skillet and then transfer them to your crockery pot slow-cooker. Add the onion, tomato sauce, chopped pickle, sherry, salt and pepper. Cover and cook on LOW for 6 to 8 hours. About 30 minutes before the end of cooking time, stir the sour cream into the pan gravy. Serve on a large platter, garnished with a beet salad.

Dutch-Style Baked Pork Chops (1)

Serves 4

4 thick pork chops	½ teaspoon nutmeg
1 lemon, peeled and cut into 4 slices	Butter or margarine
	Juice of 1 lemon
1½ teaspoons salt	½ cup bread crumbs
½ teaspoon pepper	

Trim excess fat from chops. Lightly grease your crockery pot slow-cooker and put the chops into it. Sprinkle each chop with some of the lemon juice, salt, pepper and nutmeg. Dot them with the butter or margarine, and top each with a slice of lemon. Cover and cook the chops on LOW for 6 to 8 hours. About 30 minutes before the end of cooking time, sprinkle the chops with the bread crumbs.

Fruit-Glazed Roast Pork (1)

Serves 6 to 8

3½-4 lbs. pork loin	2 cups mashed pears or quinces
1 tablespoon flour	
1 teaspoon salt	¼ cup brown sugar
1 teaspoon dry mustard	¼ teaspoon cinnamon
¼ teaspoon pepper	¼ teaspoon ground cloves

Trim excess fat from the meat. Combine the

flour with the salt, mustard and pepper. Rub this mixture all over the roast. Put the meat on a trivet in your crockery pot slow-cooker. Combine the pears or quinces with the brown sugar, cinnamon and cloves. Spread this mixture over the loin of pork. Cover and cook on LOW for 6 to 8 hours.

Roast Loin of Pork (1)

Serves 6

5 lbs. pork loin roast
2 cloves garlic, slivered
1 teaspoon thyme
1 teaspoon coarse salt
12 small new potatoes

6 carrots, quartered lengthwise
12 small white onions
½ cup water

Trim any excess fat from the pork roast. Cut slits and insert tiny slivers of garlic under the surface of the meat. Rub the roast with thyme and salt. Place the potatoes, carrots and onions in the bottom of your crockery pot slow-cooker and put the pork loin on top of them. Add the water. Cover and cook on LOW for 8 to 10 hours. Let the roast rest on a hot platter for about 15 minutes before serving. Serve with apple slices sautéed in butter and sprinkled lightly with sugar, a tossed green salad and a chilled dry white wine.

Sweet & Pungent Roast Pork Loin (1)

Serves 6

4 lbs. loin of pork, boneless, in 1 piece
10 dried apricots
3 tablespoons apricot jam

1 tablespoon apricot brandy
½ cup plus 2 tablespoons water
15 chestnuts, cooked and minced

Trim the excess fat from the pork loin roast. Cut slits in the outside, about 2 inches apart and 1½ inches deep, and stuff them with the apricots. Put the pork loin on a trivet in the crockery pot slow-cooker and cover it with a mixture of the jam, brandy, and 2 tablespoons of water. Sprinkle the minced chestnuts over the roast. Add the ½ cup of water, cover, and cook on LOW for 8 to 10 hours. Serve with buttered broccoli, spicy applesauce, and beer.

Pork Chops in Orange Marinade (1)

Serves 6

6 large loin pork chops	Rind of 1 lemon, grated
1 cup orange juice	2 tablespoons honey

Trim off excess fat from the chops. Mix the orange juice, lemon rind and honey. Pour half of the marinade into your crockery pot slow-cooker, put in the chops and pour the balance of the marinade over them. Cover and cook for 6 to 8 hours. Serve with baked beans, buttered turnip greens and beer.

Pork Chops in Red Wine (1)

Serves 4

4 large loin pork chops	½ teaspoon basil
1 tablespoon butter or margarine	¼ teaspoon thyme
1 teaspoon salt	6 shallots, chopped (or green onion bulbs)
½ teaspoon pepper	1 cup dry red wine
½ teaspoon paprika	

Trim the fat from the pork chops and brown them in the butter in a heavy skillet. Transfer them to your crockery pot slow-cooker and sprinkle them with the salt, pepper, paprika, basil and thyme. Top with the chopped shallots or white parts of green onions and pour the wine over the chops. Cover and cook on LOW for 6 to 8 hours. Serve with buttered cooked spinach, spiced peaches and a dry red wine.

Pork Chops with Apple Brandy (1)

Serves 6

6 large loin pork chops	⅛ teaspoon mace
2 large apples, peeled and sliced	¼ teaspoon nutmeg
	1 teaspoon salt
2 tablespoons water	½ teaspoon pepper
4 tablespoons apple brandy	½ teaspoon honey

Trim the fat from the chops and brown them on all sides in a heavy skillet. Put the apples, water and 2 tablespoons of the brandy in the bottom of the crockery pot slow-cooker. Sprinkle with the mace, nutmeg, salt and pepper. Stir in the honey. Arrange the chops in the pot. Cover and cook on LOW for 6 to 8 hours. Remove the chops to a hot serving platter. Add the remaining 2 tablespoons of brandy to the pan gravy, stir well and pour it over the chops. Serve with buttered broccoli, mashed sweet potatoes and a chilled sauterne.

Pennsylvania Dutch Scrapple (1)

Serves 12 to 16

2 lbs. pork neck bones	Salt and pepper to taste
1 large onion, diced fine	2½ cups corn meal

Put the neck bones, onion, and salt and pepper to taste into the crockery pot slow-cooker. Add enough water to cover well. Cover the cooker and cook on LOW for 7 to 12 hours. Remove the neck bones from the stock and strip off the meat. Return the meat to the stock and discard the bones. Stir in the corn meal, return the cover, and cook on LOW for 6 to 8 hours. About here, you ought to taste and adjust for seasonings; it's your last chance. Lightly oil or butter 2 loaf pans and pour the scrapple into them. Chill overnight. When ready to use, cut into ½-inch slices and fry until browned on both sides.

Ham with Cherry Sauce (1)

Serves 6 to 12

3 to 5 lbs. canned ham, with gelatin removed

½ cup cherry jelly (or apple)

2 teaspoons prepared mustard

4 tablespoons dry white wine

3 tablespoons corn-starch

1 can (20 oz.) cherry pie filling

Trim excess fat. Score the ham in a diamond pattern and put it into your crockery pot slow-cooker on a trivet. Mix together the jelly, mustard and 1 tablespoon of the wine, then spread this glaze over the top of the ham. Cover and cook on LOW for 6 to 12 hours, depending on the weight of the ham. About an hour before serving, raise the temperature to HIGH and baste the ham with the pan juices and glaze. Then transfer the ham to a warm platter and keep it hot. Combine the cornstarch and the 3 tablespoons of white wine into a paste. Add this paste and the pie filling to the pan juices in the crockery pot. Mix well. Cook on HIGH until the sauce is smooth and thick. Pour about half of the sauce over the ham and serve the rest on the side.

Ham Slice with Oranges (1)

Serves 4

2-3 sweet potatoes,
peeled and sliced
1/4-in. thick
1 ham slice (1-in.
thick), cut in serving
portions
3 seedless oranges,
peeled and sliced thin

3 tablespoons frozen
orange juice
concentrate
3 tablespoons honey
1/3 cup brown sugar
2 tablespoons corn-
starch

Put the sweet potatoes at the bottom of your
crockery pot slow-cooker. Arrange the ham slices
over them, then a layer of orange slices. Combine
the orange juice concentrate (thawed), honey,
brown sugar and cornstarch into a thin paste and
spread it lightly over the oranges. Cover the
crockery pot and cook on LOW for 7 to 10 hours.

Baked Lamb Chops with Vegetables (1)

Serves 6

6 large lamb shoulder
chops
1 tablespoon butter or
margarine
6 potatoes, peeled and
sliced

2 teaspoons salt
1/2 teaspoon pepper
1/2 teaspoon paprika
2 cups canned
tomatoes, chopped

Brown the chops all over in the butter, using a
heavy skillet. Lightly grease your crockery pot
slow-cooker and put 3 chops into it. Cover with
half of the potato slices. Season with half of the
salt, pepper and paprika. Spoon half of the tomatoes over the potato layer. Add the last 3 lamb
chops, the remaining potato slices, seasonings,
and tomatoes. Cover and cook on LOW for 6 to
8 hours.

Lamb Chops with Orange Sauce (1)

Serves 4 to 6

8 rib lamb chops, trimmed of fat
2 tablespoons oil
½ cup orange juice
2 tablespoons honey
2 teaspoons salt
2 tablespoons corn-starch
1 teaspoon grated orange rind

Brown the lamb chops in the oil in a heavy skillet, then drain off all the fat you can. Mix together the orange juice, honey, salt, cornstarch and orange rind. Coat the chops with this mixture and put them into your crockery pot slow-cooker. Cover and cook on LOW for 6 to 8 hours. If the sauce is not as thick as you'd like, remove the chops and keep them warm, then add a mixture of 2 tablespoons cornstarch and ¼ cup water to the pan juices. Set the indicator on HIGH and cook and stir continuously until the sauce is thick and transparent.

Lamb Chops Hotel Crillon (1)

Serves 4 to 8

8 loin lamb chops
1 tablespoon flour
1 teaspoon salt
¼ teaspoon pepper
2 tablespoons butter or margarine
8 pearl onions, peeled
1 can (4 oz.) sliced mushrooms
3 medium potatoes, peeled and sliced
1 cup dry white wine
3 tablespoons finely chopped chives

Dust the chops lightly with a mixture of the flour, salt and pepper. Brown them in the butter in a heavy skillet. Put the onions, mushrooms, and potatoes into your crockery pot slow-cooker, then put the lamb chops on top. Add the wine. Cover and cook on LOW for 6 to 8 hours. Add a sprinkling of the chives just before serving.

Lamb Stew (1)

Serves 4 to 6

¼ cup olive or salad oil
2 lbs. lean lamb, cubed
3 onions, diced
1 clove garlic, crushed
1 teaspoon salt

½ teaspoon pepper
2 cups canned tomatoes
½ teaspoon oregano
1 teaspoon sugar

Heat the oil in a heavy skillet and brown the lamb cubes on all sides. Transfer the browned meat to your crockery pot slow-cooker. Sauté the onions and garlic in the same skillet until the onions are golden. Add the salt, pepper, tomatoes, oregano and sugar. Stir and cook until the mixture is well blended, then pour it over the lamb cubes, cover, and cook on LOW for 10 to 12 hours.

Roast Shoulder of Lamb (1)

Serves 4 to 6

2 onions, sliced
1 clove garlic, minced
¼ cup olive or salad oil
4 lbs. rolled shoulder
   of lamb
¼ cup flour
½ teaspoon salt
¼ teaspoon pepper

½ teaspoon paprika
1 cup water
¼ cup vinegar
¼ cup ketchup
2 tablespoons brown
   sugar
1 teaspoon worcester-
   shire sauce

Using a heavy skillet, sauté the onions and garlic in the oil. Set them aside. Trim all excess fat from the lamb roast. Combine the flour, salt, pepper and paprika. Rub this mixture into the surface of the lamb roast. Sear the meat on all sides in the skillet, then transfer it to your crockery pot slow-cooker. In the skillet, combine the water, vinegar, ketchup, brown sugar, worcestershire sauce, sautéed onions and garlic. Stir well over heat until the ingredients are well blended. Pour sauce over lamb roast. Cover and cook on LOW for 7-9 hours, or on HIGH for 4-5 hours.

Stuffed Shoulder of Lamb (1)

Serves 6 to 8

3-4 lbs. boneless lamb
  shoulder
½ lb. bulk pork sausage
1 medium onion, diced
1 tablespoon parsley
  flakes
½ teaspoon marjoram
½ teaspoon basil

½ teaspoon oregano
1 clove garlic, crushed
2 sliced onions
2 ribs celery, sliced
2 carrots, diced
Brown-Quick or
  Kitchen Bouquet
Salt and pepper to taste

Trim off all excess fat from the meat. Brown the sausage in a skillet together with the diced onion, then drain off the fat. Combine the sausage mixture with the parsley, marjoram, basil, oregano and garlic. Spread the lamb with this mixture on one surface, roll it up, and close it with skewers or twine. Put the onion slices, celery and carrots into the crockery pot slow-cooker. Rub the lamb with Brown-Quick or Kitchen Bouquet, and sprinkle it with salt and pepper to taste. Cover the pot and cook on LOW for 10 to 12 hours. Serve with the pan juices poured over as a sauce.

Greek Lamb Stew (1)

Serves 6

3 lbs. boneless lean
  lamb, cut in 1-in.
  cubes
¼ cup flour
2 teaspoons salt
¼ teaspoon pepper
2 medium onions, diced
2 cloves garlic, crushed
1 bay leaf
2 tablespoons parsley
  flakes
¼ teaspoon saffron

1 teaspoon crystalized
  ginger
½ cup beef stock (see
  index), or bouillon
2 cups whole canned
  tomatoes
1 cup raisins
¾ cup blanched almonds
1 tablespoon butter or
  margarine
Chopped parsley
Yellow rice (see index)

Brown the lamb in a heavy skillet, then transfer it to the crockery pot slow-cooker, together with the flour, salt, pepper, onions and garlic; then mix thoroughly together. Add the bay leaf, parsley flakes, saffron, ginger, stock, tomatoes and raisins. Cover and cook on LOW for 8 to 12 hours. In a small pan, toast the almonds in the butter until golden. Serve this stew sprinkled with toasted almonds and chopped fresh parsley, with yellow rice on the side.

Lamb Shanks with Split Peas (1)

Serves 4 to 6

1 cup dried split green peas	2 carrots, diced fine
3 lbs. lamb shanks	2 ribs celery, diced fine
1 large onion, diced fine	2½ cups beef stock (see index) or bouillon
	Salt and pepper to taste

Soak the peas in 2 cups of water overnight or longer. Under the broiler flame, brown the lamb shanks well to render off all fat. In your crockery pot slow-cooker, combine the peas, onion, carrots, celery, stock, and salt and pepper to taste, mixing together thoroughly. Add the lamb shanks, sinking them in the liquid. Cover the cooker and cook on LOW for 10 to 12 hours.

Polish Sausages and Cabbage (1)

Serves 4

½ head of cabbage, coarsely shredded	1 large onion, sliced thin
1 medium potato, diced	1½ lbs. Polish sausage, in 1-in. pieces
1 teaspoon salt	2 cups chicken stock or bouillon (see index)
½ teaspoon caraway seed	

© Lorillard 1975

C'mon

Come for the filter.   You'll stay for the taste.

19 mg. "tar," 1.2 mg. nicotine av. per cigarette, FTC Report Apr. '75.

Warning: The Surgeon General Has Determined That Cigarette Smoking Is Dangerous to Your Health.

© Lorillard 1975

I'd heard enough to make me decide one of two things: quit or smoke True.

I smoke True.

The low tar, low nicotine cigarette.
Think about it.

King Regular: 11 mg. "tar", 0.6 mg. nicotine,
King Menthol: 12 mg. "tar", 0.7 mg. nicotine, 100's
Regular: 13 mg. "tar", 0.7 mg. nicotine, 100's Menthol: 13 mg.
"tar", 0.8 mg. nicotine, av. per cigarette, FTC Report April '75.

Warning: The Surgeon General Has Determined
That Cigarette Smoking Is Dangerous to Your Health.

Line the bottom of your crockery pot slow-cooker with the shredded cabbage, diced potato and caraway seed, mixed together. Add the onion slices and sausage slices. Pour the chicken stock over everything and mix lightly. Cover the crockery pot and cook on LOW for 6 to 10 hours. Serve with an assortment of condiments and boiled new potatoes, if they are in season.

Frankfurter Stew, Italian-Style (1)

Serves 6

1 cup spaghetti, in 1-in. pieces
1 tablespoon olive or salad oil
2 beef bouillon cubes
2½ cups boiling water
½ teaspoon oregano
¼ teaspoon basil

6 large frankfurters or knockwurst, ea. cut in quarters
½ lb. small zucchini squash, sliced very thin
¼ cup tomato paste
1 teaspoon sugar

Cook the spaghetti according to the directions on the package, but only until barely tender. Drain, then toss in the oil. Dissolve the bouillon cubes in the boiling water. Put the spaghetti into the crockery pot slow-cooker, together with the bouillon, oregano, basil, franks, zucchini slices, tomato paste and sugar. Mix well. Set the temperature control on LOW, cover, and cook for 6 to 8 hours.

CHAPTER FOUR
POULTRY, FISH AND EGGS

Poached Chicken (2)

Serves 4 to 6

1 chicken (3½ lbs.), with giblets
3 ribs celery with leaves, chopped fine
3 medium carrots, chopped fine
1 bunch scallions (use the white parts and a little of the green), chopped, or 1 medium onion, chopped
1 large or 2 medium leeks (white parts only), chopped
1 medium parsnip, chopped (optional)
1 handful fresh parsley, chopped (or 1 tablespoon dried parsley flakes)
2 teaspoons salt
½ teaspoon pepper

Start the night before by putting into your crockery pot slow-cooker the celery, carrots, scallions, leeks, parsnip, parsley, salt and pepper. Add 3 cups of water, cover and cook on LOW overnight. Come morning, wash and dry the chicken carefully and put it into the slow-cooker, along with 1 cup of water. Cover and cook on LOW for 4 hours. After that, turn off the heat, but do not uncover. Allow the chicken to cool completely in the pot. When cold, serve whole or sliced, or as part of another cooked dish. The meat will all be juicy and tender. Note that this does not allow enough cooking time to permit you to be away all day—unless you use an appliance timer that will turn on after you leave the house, and turn off at the proper time.

Chicken Antonia (1)

Serves 4

1 broiler (2½-3 lbs.), cut up
3 tablespoons olive or salad oil
2 carrots, sliced thin
2 onions, chopped fine
4 celery ribs, diced
3 slices ham, diced
1 green or red pepper, cut in slivers

½ lb. whole fresh mushrooms
2 teaspoons cornstarch
½ teaspoon curry powder
1 teaspoon paprika
Salt and pepper to taste
1 cup chicken stock (or bouillon)
3 tablespoons dry port wine (optional)

Brown the chicken pieces in hot oil in a heavy skillet, along with the carrots, onions, celery, ham and peppers. Add the mushrooms and sauté lightly. Transfer all these ingredients to your crockery pot slow-cooker. Sprinkle in the cornstarch, curry powder, paprika, and salt and pepper to taste. Add the chicken stock. Cover the crockery pot and cook on LOW for 5 to 7 hours, or until the chicken is tender. Stir in the port, raise the temperature to HIGH, and cook for another 5 to 10 minutes, covered.

Chicken Catalan (1)

Serves 4 to 6

1 fryer (3-4 lbs.), cut up
4 tablespoons butter or margarine
Salt and pepper to taste
2 or 3 garlic cloves, crushed
3 lemons (unpeeled), cut into thin slices

¼ teaspoon crushed dried thyme
1 bay leaf
1 cup chicken stock (or bouillon)
1 tablespoon cornstarch
¼ cup cold heavy cream (or evaporated milk)

Lightly brown the chicken pieces in the butter in a heavy skillet. Transfer the browned pieces to your crockery pot slow-cooker and add the salt, pepper, garlic, lemon slices, thyme, bay leaf and chicken stock. Cover the crockery pot and cook on LOW for 6 to 8 hours. Remove the chicken pieces to a warm platter and arrange the lemon slices over them. Keep the platter warm in the oven. Now, raise the crockery pot temperature to HIGH, stir the cornstarch together with the cream, and add that mixture to the sauce in the pot. Continue to stir and cook, uncovered, until the sauce is creamy and transparent. Strain the finished sauce over the chicken.

Hajdusagi Csirke Tokany
[Hungarian Chicken Fricassee with Bacon] (1)
Serves 6

2 small chickens (2½ lbs. ea.), ea. cut into 8 pieces	1½ teaspoons pepper
	½ teaspoon thyme
1½ teaspoons salt	1 clove garlic, stuck on a toothpick
¼ lb. smoked bacon cut in ¼-in. dice (slab or thick-sliced bacon)	2 small canned tomatoes, peeled
1 large onion, chopped fine	½ cup dry white wine

Wash and dry the chicken pieces. In a small saucepan, put the backs, necks, wingtips, gizzards, hearts and ½ teaspoon of the salt (save the livers for another dish). Add cold water to cover, cover the saucepan, and simmer for 20 to 30 minutes. Strain this stock and set it in reserve. In a large skillet, fry the bacon until it begins to render fat. Sauté the chopped onion until it is translucent, then remove it from the skillet. Sauté the chicken pieces in this fat only until they are a golden

103

color all over. Transfer the chicken to your crockery pot slow-cooker. Sprinkle it with the remaining teaspoon of salt, the pepper and the thyme. Pour ½ cup of the reserved chicken giblet stock into the skillet and stir, scraping up any browned bits on the bottom, then pour it all over the chicken. Add the garlic, tomatoes, wine and another ½ cup of the stock. Cover the crockery pot and cook on LOW for 5 to 7 hours. Discard the garlic and skim off any excess fat. The sauce should be rather thick. If not, remove the chicken to a warm platter, turn up the temperature to HIGH and cook uncovered until the sauce thickens.

Sult Csirke [Hungarian Roast Chicken] (1)

Serves 6 to 8

1 roasting chicken (approx. 5 lbs.)	½ teaspoon marjoram
1½ teaspoons salt	2 shallots (or 1 small onion)
2 tablespoons butter or margarine	Thick slices of fat bacon
	1 tablespoon oil

Wash the chicken inside and outside. Dry thoroughly. Make a stock with the neck, heart and gizzard (saving the liver for another dish), cooking them in a small saucepan in water to cover with ½ teaspoon of the salt for ½ hour. Rub the cavity and skin of the chicken with the remaining salt. Put the butter, marjoram, shallots or onion, in the cavity. Wrap the chicken in bacon, making sure to cover the breastbone and joints. Put the chicken on a trivet in your crockery pot slow-cooker. Cover and cook on HIGH for 1 hour. Remove the bacon. Cover and cook on LOW for 6 to 8 hours, or until the chicken is tender. Remove the chicken to a warm platter. Skim off most of

the fat from the juices in the crockery pot. Pour 1
cup of the hot chicken stock from the giblets into
the pot, raise the temperature to HIGH, stir well,
cover, and cook for 15 to 20 minutes.

Coq au Vin [French Chicken in Wine] (1)

Serves 4

1 fryer (3 lbs.), cut
up
¼ cup butter or
margarine (or
chicken fat)
1 medium onion,
chopped
4 carrots, diced
1 clove garlic, minced
2 tablespoons flour
2 cups dry red wine

1 small bay leaf
1 tablespoon minced
parsley
¼ teaspoon ground
savory
¼ teaspoon thyme
1½ teaspoons salt
¼ teaspoon pepper
1 can (4 oz.) button
mushrooms, drained

Wash and dry the chicken pieces thoroughly. If
you have a cholesterol problem or are concerned
about extra calories, remove most of the skin and
underlying fat. Melt the butter in a heavy skillet
and brown the chicken pieces all over. Transfer
them to your crockery pot slow-cooker. Sauté the
onions, carrots, and garlic until the onions are
light brown. Stir in the flour well, then gradually
stir in the wine. Add the bay leaf, savory, parsley,
thyme, salt and pepper. Mix the sauce well and
pour it over the chicken in the crockery pot. Cover
and cook on LOW for 6 to 8 hours. Increase the
temperature to HIGH, stir in the mushrooms,
cover, and cook for 15 minutes more.

Csirke Paprikas
[Hungarian Chicken Paprika] (1)

Serves 6

2 small chickens (2½ lbs. ea.), ea. cut in 8 pieces

1½ teaspoons salt

¼ cup chicken fat (or oil)

1 large onion, chopped fine

2 teaspoons paprika

3 small canned tomatoes, peeled

1 medium green pepper, cut in ½-in. strips

½ cup sour cream, at room temperature (or thick yogurt)

Galuska Dumplings (see index)

Hungarian Cucumber Salad (see index)

Wash and dry the chicken pieces. Save the livers for another recipe. Into a small saucepan put the backs, necks, wingtips, gizzards, hearts and ½ teaspoon of salt. Add cold water to cover, cover the pan, and simmer for 20 to 30 minutes. Heat the fat in a heavy skillet and sauté the onion until translucent. Add the chicken pieces and sauté them only until yellow all over. Transfer the chicken to the crockery pot slow-cooker, placing the breasts and thighs on the bottom, the tomatoes and green pepper strips in the middle, the legs and wings on top. Pour ½ cup of the chicken stock into the frying pan, along with 1 teaspoon of salt and the paprika. Stir well, scraping up the browned bits from the bottom of the pan. Pour the sauce over the chicken in the crockery pot and add enough stock to come halfway up the layers of chicken. Cover the pot and cook on LOW for 5 to 7 hours, or until the chicken is tender. Mix a little of the stock into the sour cream and stir this mixture carefully into the pot. Raise the temperature to HIGH and cook for another 15 minutes—but don't let the sauce boil. To serve, place the chicken on a warm platter and spoon the sauce over it. A traditional *Csirke Paprikas* must be served with lots of Galuska (dumplings) and a Hungarian Cucumber Salad. See the index for these receipes.

Galuska [Hungarian Soft Dumplings] (4)

Serves 6

3 cups flour
1½ teaspoons salt
3 eggs

2 tablespoons butter, margarine, or oil

Combine the flour and salt together in a large mixing bowl. Mix well. Add the eggs. Beat with a wooden spoon. Add as much cold water as is required to hold the dough together—about ½ cup. Beat with vigor until the dough comes away from the sides of the bowl and starts to blister on the surface, then let it rest for 45 minutes. Turn the dough out onto a wet breadboard and cut off pieces about ½-inch long and as thick as a pencil. Drop these pieces into a large kettle of boiling water. The *galuska* will be done within seconds after they rise to the surface. Drain them in a colander, or skim them off the surface with a slotted or perforated spoon. Put them into a bowl, add the butter, margarine, or oil, and serve hot with *Csirke Paprikas* (Hungarian Chicken Paprika).

Brunswick Stew (1)

Serves 6

1 fryer (3½ lbs.),
   cut up
1½ teaspoons salt
¼ teaspoon pepper
2 tablespoons fat
1 large onion, chopped
1 cup water
1 can (16 oz.)
   tomatoes
1 tablespoon worcester-
   shire sauce

⅓ cup sherry
1 pkg. (10 oz.) frozen
   lima beans, slightly
   thawed
1 cup okra, sliced
   (canned, frozen or
   fresh)
1 pkg. (10 oz.) frozen
   cut corn
½ cup fine dry bread
   crumbs

Wash and dry the chicken pieces. Season with the salt and pepper. Heat the fat in a heavy skillet and sauté the onion. Brown the chicken pieces lightly all over. Transfer the chicken and onions to your crockery pot slow-cooker and add the water, tomatoes, worcestershire, sherry, lima beans and fresh okra. Frozen or canned okra should be added later. Cover the crockery pot and cook on LOW for 6 to 8 hours. At this point, add canned or frozen okra. Add the bread crumbs and corn and mix well. Cover the pot and raise temperature to HIGH. Cook for another 15 to 20 minutes.

Chicken Montmorency (1)

Serves 4

1 fryer (3 lbs.),
   cut up
1¼ teaspoons salt
¼ teaspoon pepper
½ teaspoon paprika
3 tablespoons butter or
   margarine
1 tablespoon flour
1 teaspoon sugar

⅛ teaspoon allspice
⅛ teaspoon cinnamon
2 cups canned black
   cherries, with
   liquid reserved
1 chicken bouillon
   cube
¼ teaspoon red food
   coloring

Wash and dry the chicken pieces thoroughly. Season with 1 teaspoon of the salt, pepper and paprika. Heat the butter in a heavy skillet and brown the chicken pieces all over. Transfer the browned chicken to your crockery pot slow-cooker. To the hot skillet, add ¼ teaspoon salt, the flour, sugar, allspice, cinnamon, reserved cherry juice, bouillon cube and food coloring. Blend all this together with the pan drippings. Pour the sauce over the chicken. Cover and cook on LOW for 7 to 9 hours, or until the chicken is tender. Turn the control to HIGH, add the cherries and cook for 10 minutes. To serve, place the chicken on a platter and pour the sauce over the pieces. It would be nice if you could get pitted black cherries or else pit them before using them in the sauce.

Huhner Frikassee [German Chicken Fricassee] (1)
Serves 6

1 roasting or stewing chicken (5 lbs.), cut up
1 large onion, diced
2 carrots, diced
3 ribs celery, diced
3 sprigs fresh parsley (or 2 teaspoons dried flakes)
8 peppercorns
2 teaspoons salt
5 cups chicken stock (or bouillon, or water)
1 bay leaf
¼ cup butter or margarine
¼ cup flour
1 egg yolk, beaten
¼ cup heavy cream (or evaporated milk)
Juice of ½ lemon
¼ teaspoon nutmeg
½ lb. sliced mushrooms
2 tablespoons butter or margarine
3 cups hot cooked rice

Wash and dry the chicken pieces thoroughly and put them into your crockery pot slow-cooker, along with the onion, carrots, celery, parsley, peppercorns, salt, stock and bay leaf. Cover and cook on

LOW for 7 to 9 hours, or until the chicken is tender. Remove the chicken, discard the skin and bones, and cut the meat into bite-size pieces. Melt the ¼ cup butter in a saucepan and blend in the flour, cooking only until the mixture bubbles, then remove the pan from the heat and slowly stir in 1¾ cups of the stock. Return the pan to the heat, cook and stir until the mixture thickens. Combine the cream with the egg and add to the sauce, stirring in well. Add the lemon juice and nutmeg. Sauté the mushrooms in the 2 tablespoons of butter and add them to the sauce. Pour the hot sauce over the chicken and serve with the hot cooked rice. Any leftover stock in the pot may be cooled and frozen to be used in another recipe.

Chicken Breasts with
Madeira Wine and Lime Juice (2)

Serves 4

Juice of 1 lime
2 tablespoons dried tarragon
¾ cup beef stock (or bouillon)
⅓ cup dry Madeira wine
⅛ teaspoon cayenne pepper
1 teaspoon salt
4 whole chicken breasts, skin removed
Lemons, quartered

In a small saucepan, combine the lime juice, tarragon, stock, wine, pepper, and salt. Simmer for 20 minutes. Put the chicken breasts into the crockery pot slow-cooker, pour the wine sauce over the chicken, cover, and cook on LOW for 4 to 6 hours, or until the chicken is tender. Serve on a platter, garnished with the lemon quarters.

Chicken Viennese (1)

Serves 6

1 fryer (4-4½ lbs.), cut up
½ cup butter or margarine
2 tablespoons sherry
1 clove garlic, minced
2 tablespoons onion, minced
3 medium tomatoes, sliced
1 tablespoon tomato paste

3 tablespoons flour
1½ cups chicken stock (or bouillon)
¼ cup shredded almonds
1 teaspoon salt
1 bay leaf
¾ cup sour cream or thick yogurt
¾ cup grated Swiss cheese

Melt the butter in a heavy skillet and brown the chicken pieces all over. Add the sherry and cook 1 minute longer. Put the browned chicken in your crockery pot slow-cooker. To the skillet, add the garlic, onion and tomatoes. Cook for 3 minutes. Remove from the heat and blend in the flour and tomato paste by stirring well. Add the chicken stock and stir over the heat until it comes to a boil. Add the almonds, salt and bay leaf. Pour this sauce over the chicken. Cover and cook on LOW for 6 to 8 hours. Remove the chicken pieces to a shallow baking pan. Add the sour cream and ½ cup of the cheese to the sauce in the crockery pot, raise the temperature to HIGH, and cook and stir until the sour cream and cheese are blended into the sauce. Pour the sauce over the chicken, sprinkle on the remaining cheese, and brown under the broiler.

Chicken with Walnuts (1)

Serves 4 to 6

1 fryer (4 lbs.), cut up
1 teaspoon salt
¼ teaspoon pepper
½ cup flour
¼ cup butter or margarine
1 cup onion, finely chopped
1 clove garlic, minced
1 teaspoon grated ginger root
1 bay leaf, crumbled

1 cup red wine
½ cup brandy (or 2½ teaspoons brandy extract)
2 cups walnut meats, finely chopped
Juice of 1 lemon
1 teaspoon grated orange peel
1 teaspoon grated lemon peel

Roll the chicken pieces in a mixture of the salt, pepper and flour. Melt the butter in a heavy skillet and brown the chicken all over. Transfer the browned pieces to your crockery pot slow-cooker. To the skillet, add the onion, garlic, ginger and bay leaf. Sauté until the onions are translucent. Add the wine, brandy, and walnuts. Mix well. Add the lemon juice, orange peel and lemon peel. Stir and cook for 5 minutes to blend flavors. Pour over the chicken in the crockery pot. Cover and cook on LOW for 6 to 8 hours. Pour the chicken and sauce into a bowl and serve hot.

Chicken Gizzards in Sauce Pietro (1)

Serves 6

¼ lb. salt pork, chopped fine
1 tablespoon olive or salad oil
1 small onion, minced
2 garlic cloves, minced

1 lb. chicken gizzards, chopped
2 parsley sprigs, minced (or 1 teaspoon dried flakes)
¼ to ½ teaspoon cayenne pepper

¼ teaspoon ground
cloves
½ teaspoon crushed
dried marjoram
½ teaspoon salt
1 cup dry red wine
2 cans (6 oz. ea.)
tomato paste

2 cups (16 oz.) canned
Italian-style
tomatoes
8 oz. thin spaghetti or
fine egg noodles
Grated Romano or
Parmesan cheese

Lightly brown the salt pork in hot oil in a heavy skillet. In your crockery pot slow-cooker, combine the pork, onion, garlic, gizzards, parsley, cayenne pepper, cloves, marjoram, salt, wine, tomato paste and tomatoes. Cover the pot and cook on LOW for 5 to 7 hours. The sauce should be fairly thick. Cook the spaghetti in a separate pot according to package directions. Sprinkle your platter with cheese, add some spaghetti, more cheese and sauce. Repeat until all are used, ending with sauce and cheese.

Duck and Orange Casserole (1)

Serves 4 to 6

1 duckling (4-4½
lbs.), cut up
2 tablespoons flour
¼ cup oil

3 large seedless
oranges, sliced
1 cup orange juice
2 tablespoons lemon
juice

Dust the duckling pieces with the flour and brown them in hot oil in a heavy skillet. Transfer the browned pieces to your crockery pot slow-cooker. Arrange the orange slices around and over the duckling pieces. Combine the orange and lemon juices and pour them over the duckling. Cover crockery pot and cook on LOW for 6 to 8 hours, or until duckling pieces are tender.

Duckling-with-a-Blush (1)

Serves 4 to 6

1 duckling (4½-5½ lbs.), cut up
2 cloves garlic
3 tablespoons flour
⅛ teaspoon celery salt
⅛ teaspoon onion salt
⅛ teaspoon paprika

3 tablespoons chicken fat, duck fat, or other shortening
2 cups stewed fresh cranberries (or 1 tall can whole cranberry sauce)

Rub each piece of duckling with the garlic. Combine the flour with the celery salt, onion salt and the paprika. Roll the duckling pieces in the flour mixture until well coated. In a heavy skillet, melt the fat and brown the pieces. Transfer the browned duckling to the slow-cooking crockery pot and top with the cranberry sauce. Cover the pot and cook on LOW for 6 to 8 hours.

Roumanian Duckling with Pickled Cucumbers (1)

Serves 4

1 duckling (4 lbs.), quartered
2 teaspoons salt
¼ teaspoon pepper
¼ cup butter, margarine, or lard
1 cup onion, chopped
1 tablespoon tomato puree

1½ cups thin Demi-glace sauce (see index)
4 pickled cucumbers, 3 inches long (see index)
½ cup sour cream (or thick yogurt)

Rub the duckling pieces with 1 teaspoon of the salt and brown them in the butter in a heavy skillet. Transfer the duckling pieces to your crockery pot slow-cooker. Cook the onion in the skillet until translucent and set aside. Pour off the excess fat from the skillet, reserving about two tablespoons in the pan. Return the onions, add the remaining salt, tomato puree, the Demi-glace sauce, and the pepper. Cook for 3 or 4 minutes, stirring and scraping the bottom of the skillet to mix the ingredients thoroughly with the browned particles. Pour this sauce over the duckling. Cover the crockery pot and cook on LOW for 6 to 8 hours. Peel the pickled cucumbers, flute them by running a fork down the sides, cut them into quarters, remove and discard the seeds, cut the cucumbers into slices and add them to the duckling in the pot. Cover the pot and cook on HIGH for 15 to 20 minutes. Arrange the duckling and sauce in a serving dish and serve the sour cream as a separate garnish.

Kaposztas Liba
[Hungarian Goose in Sauerkraut] (1)

Serves 4

2 lbs. fresh sauerkraut	1 goose breast, skinned and boned (use the hindquarters in recipe for Goose in Beans; see index)
3 tablespoons goose or chicken fat (or oil)	
½ cup onion, finely chopped	
1½ teaspoons paprika	2 cloves garlic, peeled and stuck on toothpicks
Goose or chicken stock (or bouillon, or water)	
1 teaspoon salt	¼ cup sour cream
	Boiled potatoes

Rinse the sauerkraut in cold water and drain. Heat the fat or oil in a heavy skillet and sauté the onions until wilted. Stir in the paprika, cooking and stirring for 2 to 3 minutes. Add ¼ cup of stock or water and the salt, and mix thoroughly. Squeeze out the sauerkraut and add it to the onion sauce, combining well. Cut the goose breast into 1-in. cubes and put them into your crockery pot slow-cooker. Pour the sauce over the meat

and mix them together. Add the garlic and enough
stock or water to come halfway up the contents.
Cover and cook on LOW for 7 to 9 hours. Remove
the garlic. Stir some of the sauerkraut and
sauce into the sour cream, then slowly pour that
mixture into the pot, stirring all the while. Increase the temperature to HIGH, cover and cook
for 15 to 20 minutes. Serve directly from the pot,
or from a large serving bowl, with the boiled
potatoes on the side.

Solet [Goose in Beans] (1)

Serves 4

1 lb. large white beans
3 tablespoons goose or
  chicken fat (or oil)
1 medium onion,
  chopped fine
1 tablespoon flour
1½ teaspoons paprika
1 teaspoon salt
3 cloves garlic, peeled
  & stuck on toothpicks

2 goose legs and hind-
  quarters (use the
  forequarters and
  breast in Goose in
  Sauerkraut; see
  index)
Goose or chicken stock
  (or bouillon, or
  water)

Wash and sort the beans, then soak them overnight in cold water. Or else, boil the beans for 5
minutes, cover them, and allow them to stand
and soak for an hour or more. Drain the beans,
reserving the liquid. Heat the fat or oil in a skillet
and sauté the onion until translucent. Sprinkle
them with the flour and paprika and cook for 3
or 4 minutes, stirring constantly. Add the salt
and ½ cup of water, mix thoroughly, then add
the beans, stirring to combine them with the
sauce. Transfer the beans and sauce to your
crockery pot slow-cooker. Bury the garlic and
the pieces of goose meat in the beans and add
enough stock or reserved bean water to cover

exactly. Cover the crockery pot and cook on LOW for 10 to 12 hours, or on HIGH for 5 to 6 hours.

Braised Turkey (1)

Serves 6 to 8

3 tablespoons butter or margarine
3 tablespoons olive or salad oil
1 turkey (9 lbs.), cut up for frying
2 medium carrots, chopped
2 ribs celery with leaves, chopped
2 medium onions, chopped
1 bay leaf
½ teaspoon thyme
3 sprigs parsley (or 1¼ teaspoons dried parsley flakes)
2 jiggers whiskey
Salt and pepper
2 cups dry white wine
Water
1 lb. fresh mushrooms (optional)

Melt the butter in a heavy skillet, add the oil and brown the turkey pieces, a few at a time. Set the cooked pieces aside in a separate dish. When there is no more turkey in the skillet, put in the carrots, celery, onions, bay leaf, thyme and parsley and brown well, stirring often. Add the whiskey and heat slightly. Ignite the alcohol, and tilt the skillet to and fro to burn off all of it. Put the vegetables into the bottom of your crockery pot slow-cooker and top them with the cooked turkey pieces, white meat last. Add salt and pepper to taste, the white wine and enough water to come halfway up the ingredients in the pot. Cover and cook on LOW for 7 to 9 hours, or until tender. Transfer the turkey to a warm platter and strain the gravy into a bowl. Skim off all fat. If you use the mushrooms, clean them gently and sauté in butter and a little lemon juice for 5 to 7 minutes. Add them to the gravy and pour it over the turkey. Warning: This recipe is suitable only for a 4½-quart or larger crockery pot slow-cooker.

Poached Breast of Turkey (1)

Serves 6 to 8

4 ribs celery with some leaves, finely chopped

2 bunches scallions (with half green parts), finely chopped

2 medium carrots, finely chopped

1 small parsnip, finely chopped (optional)

3 tablespoons fresh parsley, chopped (or 1½ tablespoons dried parsley flakes)

2 teaspoons salt

½ teaspoon pepper

1 medium-size breast of turkey

4 cups water

Into the crockery pot slow-cooker, put the celery, scallions, carrots, parsnip, parsley, salt, pepper and breast of turkey. Add the water and cover. Cook for 7 to 9 hours on LOW, or until the meat is tender. If you are serving the turkey cold, allow it to cool in the crockery pot. Remove the skin before serving. This poached turkey can also be used for sandwiches and in other cooked dishes.

Curried Creamed Chicken (3)

Serves 4

1 teaspoon curry powder

1 cup beer

4 tablespoons chili sauce

2 cans cream of mushroom soup, undiluted

2 cups diced leftover cooked chicken

Blend together the curry powder, beer, sauce and soup. Heat thoroughly in a saucepan. Add the diced chicken, stir, and simmer for 3 to 5 minutes. Serve with buttered noodles, mashed potatoes, or rice.

118

Chicken-Stuffed Tomatoes (3)

Serves 4

4 large firm tomatoes
1 teaspoon salt
1 cup chopped cooked
chicken (see index)
½ cup cracker crumbs
1 egg
1 tablespoon cream
(or evaporated milk)

1 teaspoon onion juice
Salt and pepper
½ teaspoon powdered
basil
1 cup chicken stock
(see index), or
bouillon
4 slices buttered toast

Cut a small slice off the top of each tomato and scoop out the pulp, reserving it for use in the stuffing. Sprinkle the insides of the tomatoes with 1 teaspoon of the salt. Remove the seeds from the reserved pulp and drain off the excess juice. Combine this pulp with the chicken, cracker crumbs, egg, cream, onion juice, salt and pepper to taste, and the basil. Mix the stuffing well and use it to stuff the cavities in the tomatoes. Set the tomatoes in a baking dish and pour the chicken stock around them. Bake at 350 degrees for 30 to 40 minutes, or until the tomatoes are just tender. During this baking period, baste several times with the chicken stock. Serve the stuffed tomatoes on slices of hot toast.

Bass Baked in Beer (2)

Serves 4

2 lbs. bass
Salt and pepper to taste
1 onion, chopped
½ cup chopped parsley
1 clove garlic, chopped
fine

1 cup canned tomatoes,
chopped
½ teaspoon tomato
paste
½ teaspoon oregano
½ cup beer

Lightly oil the inside of your crockery pot slow-cooker and put the bass inside. Sauté the onion and spread it on top of the fish. Add the parsley and garlic. Combine the tomatoes, tomato paste, oregano and beer, and pour it over the bass. Cover the crockery pot and cook on LOW for 3½ to 4 hours. The fish should flake apart easily when it is completely cooked.

Stewed Sole with Tomatoes (2)

Serves 4

1 large onion, sliced
2 tablespoons butter or margarine
2 bouillon cubes, crushed (or 2 teaspoons instant bouillon crystals)
1 cup white wine
1 cup fish stock (see index)
3 oz. tomato paste
2 lbs. fillet of sole
2 tablespoons flour
Salt and pepper to taste

Brown the onions in 1 tablespoon of the butter in a heavy skillet. In your crockery pot slow-cooker, combine the bouillon, wine, stock and tomato paste. Cut the fish fillets into serving-size pieces and add them to the cooker. Cover and cook on LOW for 2½ to 3 hours. Melt the remaining tablespoon of butter in a pan, mix in the flour and a little broth to make a thin paste, then stir the mixture into the cooker. Cover and cook on HIGH for 20 to 30 minutes.

Sole in White Wine (2)

Serves 4

2 lbs. fillet of sole
2 tablespoons butter or margarine
1 cup fish stock (see index)
½ cup sliced mushrooms
Salt and pepper to taste
1 cup white wine
2 tablespoons flour
2 egg yolks, beaten

Wash and dry the fillets. Cut them into serving-size pieces and put them into your crockery pot slow-cooker with 1 tablespoon of the butter. Add the fish stock, wine, salt and pepper to taste. Cover and cook on LOW for 2½ to 3 hours, or until fish flakes easily. Transfer the fish to a warm platter in your oven. Raise the crockery pot temperature to HIGH. Make a thin paste of the flour and some of the stock from the pot. Stir this paste into the pot, blending thoroughly. Cover and cook on HIGH for about 15 minutes. Then, add the beaten egg yolks to the sauce, mix well, and pour the sauce over the fish on the platter. Serve hot.

Carp in Red Cabbage (2)

Serves 4 to 6

1 head red cabbage, shredded
1 tablespoon butter or margarine
1 large onion, chopped
1 tablespoon flour
1 cup red wine
Salt and pepper to taste
1 tablespoon sugar
Juice of 1 lemon
2-3 lbs. carp

Put the cabbage into a colander and pour boiling water over it. Brown the onion in the butter in a heavy skillet. Sprinkle flour over the onion, then stir in the wine. Transfer the cabbage to the crockery cooker and add salt and pepper to taste, the lemon juice, sugar and the onion-wine sauce. Stir together well. Cut the carp into serving-size pieces and mix them gently with the cabbage. Cover the cooker and cook on LOW for 3 to 4 hours.

Carp in Mushroom Sauce (2)

Serves 4

2 lbs. carp
¼ cup butter or
  margarine, melted

Salt and pepper to taste
Mushroom sauce (see
  index)

Clean and dry the fish, then place it in your slow-cooking crockery pot. Season to taste with salt and pepper. Pour the melted butter over the fish. Cover the crockery cooker and cook on LOW for 2½ to 3 hours. Pour mushroom sauce over the fish, re-cover the cooker, and cook on HIGH for 30 minutes.

Badacsonyi Fogas
[Hungarian Fish Fillets in Green Pepper & Tomato Sauce] (2)

Serves 6

3 lbs. fish fillets (any
  fish)
Salt to taste
2 tablespoons olive or
  salad oil
1 small onion, chopped
  fine
1 tablespoon chopped
  parsley
½ cup wine
  (optional)

4 fresh tomatoes (or 4
  canned tomatoes),
  drained
1 medium green
  pepper, cut in ½-in.
  strips
2 tablespoons flour
1 teaspoon paprika
1 cup fish stock
  (see index)
Boiled potatoes

Clean and dry the fish fillets, salt them, and put them into your crockery pot slow-cooker, having lightly oiled the inside first. Sauté the onions until wilted. Add the parsley, wine, tomatoes and green peppers, and sauté for 2 to 3 more minutes; then sprinkle with the flour. Cook for 2 or 3 minutes more, until the flour begins to brown.

Stir in the paprika; then add the fish stock, stir, and cook until well blended. Pour the sauce over the fillets in the crockery cooker. Cover and cook on LOW for 2½ to 3 hours. Serve hot with plain boiled potatoes.

Ribarski Gjuvec
[Bulgarian Fish with Vegetables] (2)

Serves 4 to 5

1 small celery root, diced
1 lb. carrots, diced
2 cloves garlic, crushed
2 onions, diced
1 lb. canned whole tomatoes, drained
½ cup dry white wine
1 bay leaf
Salt and pepper to taste
2 lbs. fish fillets (any kind)
½ cup bread crumbs
2 tablespoons butter or margarine
¼ cup grated walnuts (optional)

Combine celery root, carrots, garlic, onion, tomatoes, wine, bay leaf, and salt and pepper to taste in the bottom of your lightly greased crockery pot slow-cooker. Cover them with the fish fillets and sprinkle with the bread crumbs or a mixture of the bread crumbs and grated walnuts. Dot the top with butter. Cover the crockery pot and bake on LOW for 3 to 4 hours, or until the fish flakes easily.

Brodet Na Bokeljski Nacin
[Yugoslavian Boka Fish Stew] (2)

Serves 4 to 6

2 lbs. fish (any kind)
2 onions, sliced
3 cloves garlic, chopped fine
¼ cup olive or salad oil
1 tablespoon flour
¼ cup water

1 tablespoon vinegar
¾ cup white wine
4 to 5 canned tomatoes, drained and crushed
Salt and pepper to taste
1 to 2 bay leaves

Clean and dry the fish, then cut it into 3-inch pieces. In a heavy skillet, sauté the onion slices and garlic together in the heated oil until golden. Add the flour; stir and cook 1 or 2 minutes. Stir in the water, vinegar and wine. Add the tomatoes, salt, pepper and bay leaves. Stir and cook for 2 minutes, or until all ingredients are well blended. Transfer the fish and sauce to your crockery pot slow-cooker. Cover and cook on LOW for 3 to 4 hours.

Brodet Na Dalmatinski Nacin
[Yugoslavian-Dalmatian Fish Stew] (2)

Serves 4 to 6

1 cup sliced onions
¼ cup olive or salad oil
2½ lbs. fish fillets (any kind)
½ lb. tomatoes, chopped (or 3 tablespoons tomato paste)

Salt and pepper to taste
1 tablespoon vinegar
½ cup dry white wine
¼ cup red wine
2 tablespoons chopped parsley
Polenta (see index)

Sauté ½ cup of the onions in heated oil in a heavy skillet and then transfer them to the bottom of your crockery pot slow-cooker. Cut the fish fillets into serving-size pieces and place them on top of the sautéed onions. Add the remaining ½ cup of sliced onions, the tomatoes (or tomato paste), pepper and salt to taste, vinegar and the wines. Cover the crockery pot and cook on LOW for 3 to 4 hours. Sprinkle with the parsley and serve with polenta or cooked rice.

Belgian Beer Waffles (4)

Serves 6

3 cups light beer	1 teaspoon vanilla
3½ cups flour	1 teaspoon lemon juice
⅓ cup salad oil	⅛ teaspoon salt
2 eggs	½ pt. whipping cream
2 tablespoons grated lemon rind	Light brown sugar

Combine in a large mixing bowl the beer, flour, oil, eggs, lemon rind, vanilla, lemon juice and salt. Beat this mixture until smooth, then let stand for 2 hours or refrigerate overnight. Spread the batter very thin over a hot buttered waffle iron and bake the waffles until they are lacy and crisp. Whip the cream. Serve each waffle with a heap of whipped cream on top and a sprinkling of light brown sugar.

Cheese Souffle (2)

Serves 4

2 cups hot water	1 teaspoon salt
1½ cups milk	6 eggs (at room temperature)
4½ tablespoons minute tapioca	⅓ teaspoon cream of tartar
1½ cups grated sharp cheddar cheese	

Put the 2 cups of hot water and a trivet into your crockery pot slow-cooker, cover the pot, and preheat it on HIGH. In a saucepan, combine the

125

milk and tapioca. Cook until the tapioca changes from white to clear granules. Remove the saucepan from the heat and add the cheese and salt. Mix well and allow to cool for at least 5 minutes. Separate the egg yolks and whites. Beat the yolks and add them to the cooled mixture. Beat the egg whites until frothy and add the cream of tartar (⅓ teaspoon is roughly ¼ teaspoon plus ⅛ teaspoon). Beat the whites more, until stiff but not dry. Fold the cheese mixture into the egg whites, using a spatula or wire whisk. Make a 2-inch collar of aluminum foil around the top of a 2-quart souffle dish (fits a 4½-5-quart crockery pot). Butter the dish lightly to prevent sticking, and pour in the mixture. Put 6 or 7 thicknesses of paper toweling over the mouth of the cooker, cover, and bake on HIGH for 3 hours—without lifting cover!—or until a knife inserted at the center comes out clean. Serve plain or with a mushroom or shrimp sauce.

CHAPTER FIVE
SAUCES AND DRESSINGS

Italian Sausage Sauce (for Pasta) (1)

Makes about 2 cups

1 lb. Italian sweet
    sausages, cut to bite-
    size pieces
1 onion, chopped
1 large can (1 lb., 12
    oz.) tomatoes
1 can (8 oz.) tomato
    paste

1 clove garlic, minced
1 teaspoon salt
½ teaspoon freshly
    ground pepper
1 bay leaf
½ teaspoon sugar
¼ teaspoon allspice
¼ teaspoon oregano

Brown the sausage in a heavy skillet, drain
well and transfer to the crockery pot slow-cooker.
To the cooker, add the onion, tomatoes, tomato
paste, garlic, salt and pepper, bay leaf, sugar,
allspice and oregano. Cover and cook on LOW
8 to 10 hours.

Neapolitan Light Tomato Sauce (1)

Makes about 7 cups

4 tablespoons minced
    ham
3 chopped onions
1 tablespoon basil

9 cups Italian canned
    plum tomatoes
    (strained)
Salt and pepper to taste

In the crockery pot slow-cooker, combine the
ham, onions, basil, tomatoes, salt and pepper.
Cover and cook on LOW 8 to 10 hours. Toss your
favorite pasta with this sauce and plenty of
grated Parmesan cheese in a large bowl.

"Monday" Spaghetti Sauce (1)

Serves 4 to 6

2 sweet Italian
sausages, cut up and
sautéed (optional)
4 cups chopped leftover
roast
1 onion, chopped
½ teaspoon dry mustard

1 tablespoon parsley,
minced
8 cups tomatoes,
pureed
½ teaspoon salt
¼ teaspoon freshly
ground black pepper

In your crockery pot slow-cooker, combine the
sausages (if used) with the roast, onion, mustard,
parsley, tomatoes, salt and pepper. Cover and
cook 8 to 10 hours on a LOW setting.

This recipe is among our family favorites. Not
only does it solve the problem of what to do with
that leftover roast beef, it is also an especially
tasty variation of a traditional Italian spaghetti
sauce.

Cook spaghetti *al dente*, drain and toss with a
liberal amount of grated Parmesan cheese. Serve
in a heated bowl with the sauce in a separate
bowl.

Sauce Espagnole (4)

Makes about 3½ cups

¼ cup butter or
margarine
½ cup onion, finely
chopped
½ cup carrot, finely
chopped
2 tablespoons parsley,
finely chopped
½ teaspoon thyme

½ bay leaf
4 tablespoons flour
1 cup dry white wine
2½ cups beef broth or
bouillon
1 tablespoon tomato
paste
⅛ teaspoon pepper
Salt to taste

Melt the butter in a 2-quart saucepan and add
the onion, carrot, parsley, thyme and bay leaf.

Stir and simmer for 12 minutes—until the vegetables are tender and begin to brown. Remove the pan from the heat and stir in the flour until it is well-blended. Return the pan to the heat and stir and simmer until the mixture becomes a hazelnut brown. Stir in the wine and the broth. Bring to a boil, reduce heat, and simmer for 30 to 40 minutes. Mix in the tomato sauce, pepper, and salt to taste. Use as is, or as a base for Demi-glace sauce.

Demi-glace Sauce (4)

Makes about 2 cups

2 cups Sauce
Espagnole (see
preceding recipe)

2 cups beef broth or
bouillon
2 tablespoons sherry

In a 2-quart saucepan, combine the Sauce Espagnole and the beef broth. Blend well. Simmer over low heat until the mixture is reduced to approximately 2 cups. Remove the pan from the heat and blend in the sherry.

I am sorry to make this a 2-step recipe: Sauce Espagnole to Sauce Demi-glace—but that's what a Demi-glace sauce is, a reduced Espagnole. At that, I cut the cooking time by quite a bit. A classical French Demi-glace takes up to several days to prepare.

Mushroom Sauce (4)

Serves 4

½ cup chopped
mushrooms
1 large onion,
chopped

3 tablespoons butter or
margarine
2 tablespoons flour
¼ teaspoon salt
1 cup milk

131

Sauté the onion and mushrooms in 1 table-spoon of the butter in a saucepan or skillet. Set aside. Melt the remaining butter in the saucepan and blend in the flour and salt, cooking until the mixture bubbles. Remove from the heat and stir in the milk gradually. Continue stirring until the mixture is smooth. Return to the heat and cook until the sauce is smooth. Add the sautéed mush-rooms and onions; then mix well. Serve with souffles, fish, veal cutlets, boiled beef, cubed steaks, or chopped meats.

Basic French Dressing (4)
Makes 1⅓ cups

⅓ cup vinegar   ½ teaspoon pepper
   (wine or cider)   1 cup olive or salad oil
¾ teaspoon salt

Mix together the vinegar, salt and pepper. Stir well. Add the oil slowly while beating thoroughly. Use a hand beater, mixer, or blender.

That's a basic French dressing. But you don't have to stop here. Add 1 tablespoon of ketchup and it's Ketchup French. Or add 2 tablespoons of Chili sauce and it's Chili Sauce French Dressing. Or add 2 tablespoons of chopped chutney and it's Chutney French. Two teaspoons of curry powder mixed in will make it Curry French Dressing. A tablespoon of chopped capers makes it Caper French Dressing. Two teaspoons of minced chives turns the basic French into Chive French Dress-ing. And, to make a Herb French Dressing, add 1 or 2 tablespoons of minced fresh tarragon, cher-vil, basil and chives (or ¼ to 1 teaspoon of each of the dried herbs). A clove of crushed garlic mixed in will turn the basic French to Garlic French. Some other French Dressings follow.

132

Lemon French Dressing (4)

Makes about ¾ cups

3 tablespoons lemon
juice
½ teaspoon salt
⅛ teaspoon pepper

¼ teaspoon sugar
¼ teaspoon dry
mustard (optional)
½ cup olive or salad oil

Mix the lemon juice well with the salt, pepper, sugar and mustard. Pour the oil in slowly, a teaspoon at a time, while beating by hand, or with an electric beater or blender.

Egg and Olive French Dressing (4)

Makes about 1⅓ cups

1 cup basic French
dressing (see index)
2 hardcooked eggs,
chopped fine

1 tablespoon pitted
olives (or pimiento-
stuffed), chopped
fine

Combine the French dressing with the chopped eggs and olives. This is a fine dressing for a mixed green salad.

Herb and Wine French Dressing (4)

Makes about 1⅓ cups

½ teaspoon salt
⅛ teaspoon pepper
1 teaspoon sugar
¼ teaspoon dry
mustard
½ cup dry white wine

1 tablespoon minced
shallots (or 1
teaspoon minced
onion)
¼ cup white wine
vinegar
½ cup olive or salad oil

Combine the salt, pepper, sugar and mustard. Stir in the wine. Add the shallots, vinegar and oil. Mix well.

133

Sherry French Dressing (4)

Makes about 2¼ cups

1 teaspoon sugar
½ teaspoon salt
1 raw egg
¼ cup vinegar

1½ cups oil (at least half olive)
½ cup sherry

Mix together the sugar, salt and egg. Add the vinegar. Then add the oil slowly while beating by hand or with an electric blender or mixer. Add the sherry in a slow stream while mixing well. To be at its best, the oil used should be at least half light olive oil. This dressing is especially suitable for a dessert salad.

Creamy Pink French Dressing (4)

Makes about 1¼ cups

1 cup basic French dressing (see index)
¼ cup ketchup

1 egg white
1 tablespoon lemon juice

Combine the basic French dressing with the ketchup, egg white, and lemon juice. Beat with a rotary or electric beater until fluffy. It's a good dressing for mixed green salads.

Vinaigrette Dressing (4)

Makes about 1½ cups

1 cup basic French dressing (see index)
2 tablespoons minced parsley
2 tablespoons minced sweet pickle

2 tablespoons minced green pepper
2 tablespoons minced chives
1 tablespoon chopped capers (optional)

Combine the basic French dressing in a cruet with the parsley, pickle, pepper, chives and capers, and shake well to mix. This is excellent on

134

freshly cooked or cold asparagus—or on artichokes.

Egg Vinaigrette Dressing (4)

Makes about 1 cup

2 hardcooked eggs
1 raw egg yolk
½ cup oil
1 teaspoon minced parsley (or cilantro)
1 teaspoon minced oregano
1 teaspoon minced chives
1 teaspoon minced thyme
2 tablespoons vinegar (or lemon juice)
½ teaspoon salt
¼ teaspoon pepper

Mash the yolks of the hardcooked eggs together with the raw egg yolk. Add the oil about a teaspoon at a time while beating steadily. Add the parsley, oregano, chives, thyme, vinegar, salt and pepper, and mix thoroughly. Chop the whites of the hardcooked eggs fine and stir them in. Try this on artichokes for a special treat!

Basic Mayonnaise (4)

Makes about 1½ cups

1 egg yolk, raw
½ teaspoon salt
½ teaspoon dry mustard (optional)
1 cup olive or salad oil
2 tablespoons vinegar (or lemon juice)

Combine the egg yolk, salt and mustard in a mixing bowl. Add the oil drop by drop while stirring with a fork or rotary beater until the mayonnaise begins to thicken. Then add the oil in a slow stream, stirring all the while. If the mayonnaise gets too thick, add a little vinegar and then go right on slowly adding the oil.

Vary this recipe in any of the following ways. Add ¾ cup chili sauce for Chili Mayonnaise. Add

⅛ teaspoon curry powder and ⅛ teaspoon paprika for Curry Mayonnaise. Add ½ teaspoon garlic salt and 1 teaspoon curry powder for Garlic-Curry Mayonnaise. Or add 3-4 drops of lemon juice and 2 teaspoons curry powder for Lemon-Curry Mayonnaise. Or ½ teaspoon dried tarragon and 1 tablespoon French dressing for a Tarragon Mayonnaise. Try adding 2 teaspoons dry mustard and 1 teaspoon wine vinegar for Mustard Mayonnaise. Or 2 tablespoons chicken stock and 1 teaspoon lemon juice for Chicken Mayonnaise. Or 2 tablespoons capers, 1 teaspoon grated onion and ½ teaspoon poultry seasoning for Caper Mayonnaise (you can leave out the poultry seasoning unless the mayonnaise is for poultry salad or cold veal salad). Other mayonnaise recipes follow.

Caraway Mayonnaise (4)

Makes about ¾ cup

½ cup basic mayonnaise (see index)
2 tablespoons vinegar
1 tablespoon grated onion

2 teaspoons caraway seeds
1 teaspoon sugar
½ teaspoon salt
⅛ teaspoon pepper

Combine the mayonnaise, vinegar, onion, caraway seeds, sugar, salt and pepper. Mix together thoroughly.

Caviar Mayonnaise (4)

Makes about 1¾ cup

1 cup basic mayonnaise (see index)
½ cup caviar
1 teaspoon lemon juice

1 tablespoon chopped onion (or chives)
2 hardcooked eggs, chopped fine

Combine the basic mayonnaise with the caviar, onion, lemon juice and chopped eggs. Mix together thoroughly. Use as a special occasion dressing for soft greens salads, or over any molded salad.

Red Caviar Mayonnaise (4)

Makes about 1½ cups

1 cup basic mayonnaise (see index)
¾ cup red caviar
Juice of ¼ lemon
1 tablespoon prepared horseradish

Into the basic mayonnaise, stir a mixture of the red caviar, lemon juice, horseradish—very gently. It's exceptionally good for egg salad.

Green Goddess Mayonnaise (4)

Makes about 2 cups

2 tablespoons finely chopped anchovies (or 1 tablespoon anchovy paste)
3 tablespoons finely chopped scallions (or chives)
⅓ cup finely chopped parsley (or cilantro)
½ cup heavy cream (or evaporated milk)
1 tablespoon lemon juice
1 tablespoon tarragon vinegar
⅛ teaspoon salt
⅛ teaspoon pepper
1 cup basic mayonnaise (see index)

Combine the anchovies, scallions, parsley, cream, lemon juice, vinegar, salt and pepper. Gently add this mixture to the basic mayonnaise and let stand in the refrigerator for several hours to blend the flavors. This is an excellent mayonnaise for crab, lobster, or any other shellfish.

Sherry Mayonnaise (4)

Makes about 2¼ cups

1 cup basic mayonnaise (see index)

¼ cup pale dry sherry
1 cup whipped cream

Combine the basic mayonnaise with the sherry and the whipped cream and use this special dressing on chicken or turkey—also on dessert-type fruit salads.

Tartare Sauce (4)

Makes about 1½ cups

1 cup basic mayonnaise (see index)

2 tablespoons finely chopped sweet pickles

2 tablespoons finely chopped green olives

2 tablespoons finely chopped parsley

2 tablespoons coarsely chopped capers

2 tablespoons minced onion (or chopped scallions)

Combine the basic mayonnaise with the pickles, olives, parsley, capers and onions. This is a fine fish accompaniment.

Thousand Island Dressing (4)

Makes about 1½ cups

1 cup basic mayonnaise (see index)

3 tablespoons chili sauce

1 tablespoon cider vinegar

1 tablespoon cream (or evaporated milk)

1 tablespoon minced green pepper

¼ cup chopped celery

1 hardcooked egg, chopped fine

¼ teaspoon salt

½ teaspoon paprika

Mix together thoroughly the basic mayonnaise, chili sauce, vinegar, cream, green pepper, celery, hardcooked egg, salt and paprika.

Bacon Salad Dressing (4)

Makes about ¾ cup

6 slices bacon
½ cup vinegar
¼ teaspoon salt

½ teaspoon sugar
½ teaspoon pepper

Fry the bacon until crisp in a heavy skillet. Remove the bacon from the skillet and reserve it. To the pan drippings, add the vinegar, salt, sugar and pepper. Heat through. Crumble the reserved bacon and add it to the dressing. Serve it warm over lettuce or raw spinach leaves as a wilted salad.

Chicken Liver Salad Dressing (4)

Makes about 1 cup

½ lb. chicken livers
2 tablespoons butter or margarine
1 medium onion, minced

4 hardcooked eggs
¼ cup basic mayonnaise (see index)
½ teaspoon salt
⅛ teaspoon pepper

Sauté the livers in the butter and then add the onion and cook until transparent. Reserve the pan drippings. Chop the livers with the hardcooked eggs and onions. Add the pan drippings, basic mayonnaise, salt and pepper. Taste and correct the seasonings. Serve on lettuce or on a mixed greens salad.

CHAPTER SIX
BEANS, RICE, VEGETABLES, SALADS AND APPETIZERS
(See Chapter 5 for salad dressings)

Beer-Baked Beans (1)

Serves 6 to 8

1 lb. navy beans	½ teaspoon dry mustard
½ lb. sliced salt pork	2 tablespoons molasses
1½ teaspoons salt	2 tablespoons ketchup
2 tablespoons brown sugar	1 onion, sliced
	1½ cups beer

Wash and drain the beans, then cover them in a pot with water and let them soak overnight. Drain off the beans and place half of them in the bottom of your slow-cooking crockery pot. Arrange half of the salt pork over these beans. Spread with half of the salt, brown sugar, dry mustard, molasses, ketchup and onion slices. Top with the rest of the salt pork, the rest of the beans and the rest of the seasonings. Pour the beer over the entire mixture. If it does not cover the beans, add more beer. Cover the crockery pot, set on LOW, and bake for 8 to 12 hours.

Breton Beans (1)

Serves 4 to 6

1½ cups dried pea beans or navy beans	1 clove garlic, minced
1 cup chicken bouillon	¼ cup melted butter or margarine
1 cup strained canned tomatoes	Salt and pepper to taste
1 onion, minced	4 pimientos, mashed

Wash beans and soak overnight in water to cover. Drain. Combine the beans with bouillon, tomatoes, onion, garlic, butter, salt, pepper and pimientos. Cook in crockery pot slow-cooker, covered, on a LOW setting for 10 to 12 hours. May be cooked on HIGH 4 to 6 hours, stirring occasionally.

Southern-Style Baked Beans (1)

Serves 6

1 lb. dried marrow
beans (large, white
beans)
1 cup water (from
soaked beans)
2 garlic cloves, minced
1 onion, diced
1 small dried hot red
pepper
1 bay leaf
3 tablespoons molasses

¼ cup ketchup
1 teaspoon powdered
mustard
½ teaspoon ground
ginger
1½ teaspoons
worcestershire
½ teaspoon salt
¼ cup firmly packed
brown sugar
¾ lb. salt pork, sliced

Soak beans in water to cover, overnight. Drain
and reserve 1 cup of the liquid. In the crockery
pot slow-cooker, combine the beans, water, cloves,
onion, red pepper and bay leaf. In a separate
bowl, mix together the molasses, ketchup, mustard, ginger, worcestershire, salt and brown
sugar and mix thoroughly with ingredients in the
crock pot. Cover and cook on LOW 10 to 12 hours.
May be cooked on HIGH 4 to 6 hours, stirring
occasionally.

Saffron Rice (1)

Serves 6 to 8

2 cups long grain
converted rice (raw)
4½ cups water

¼ cup melted butter or
margarine
¼ teaspoon saffron
2 teaspoons salt

Combine the rice, water, melted butter, saffron
and salt in your crockery pot slow-cooker and
mix well. Cover, set on LOW, and cook for 8 to
9 hours.

Yellow Rice (1)

Serves 6 to 8

2 cups long grain
converted rice (raw)
4½ cups water
¼ cup melted butter or
margarine

½ cup brown sugar
2 teaspoons salt
2½ teaspoons turmeric
1 cup raisins

Combine the rice, water, melted butter, brown sugar, salt, turmeric and raisins in your crockery pot slow-cooker. Stir together well, cover, and cook on LOW for 8 to 9 hours. This is an excellent accompaniment to Greek Lamb Stew.

Polenta [Corn Meal Mush] (4)

Serves 4 to 6

1 cup yellow corn meal
5 cups cold water

1 teaspoon salt

Soak the corn meal for an hour or more in 1 cup of the cold water. In a heavy saucepan, or the top of a double boiler, bring the other four cups of water to a boil. Add the soaked corn meal, stirring continuously. Cook and stir for 2 minutes. Cover, reduce heat, and simmer for 30 to 45 minutes, or until done. Serve with Dalmatian Fish Stew (see index).

Fried Tomatoes (4)

Serves 4

3 large firm tomatoes
Salt
⅔ cup pancake mix

6 tablespoons milk
Oil for deep frying
Grated Parmesan cheese

Core the tomatoes and slice them into thick wedges. Sprinkle the wedges lightly with salt. Blend together the pancake mix and the milk to form a smooth batter (you may need more milk than specified, depending upon the mix used). Dip the tomatoes into the batter and fry them in hot deep fat (375 degrees), until golden brown, turning only once. Remove the fried tomatoes from the fat with a slotted spoon and let them drain on several thicknesses of paper toweling or paper napkins. Sprinkle them with the Parmesan cheese and serve while still warm.

Pickled Cucumbers (4)

Makes 1 quart jar

Cucumbers (3 to 3½ inches long)
1 tablespoon coarse salt
1 teaspoon brown sugar

1 tablespoon vinegar
3 cloves garlic
3 bay leaves
Dried dillweed

Pack the cucumbers into quart jars and add spices to each jar in the amounts shown above. Also add to each jar as much boiled water (slightly cooled) as will fill the jar to the top. Adjust rubber rings and covers but do not seal. Keep the jars at room temperature until the fermentation stops and the liquid in the jars becomes cloudy. Then tighten the covers and store the jars in a cool place. Fermentation will be speeded up if the jars are placed in the sun. The pickles will be ready to eat within ten days—depending upon whether you like "new" pickles or well-pickled pickles. Use these pickles in the Roumanian Duckling with Pickled Cucumbers recipe (see index).

Chiles Rellenos (2)

Serves 6

1 lb. ground beef (lean)
½ cup chopped onion
½ teaspoon salt
¼ teaspoon pepper
2 cans (4 oz. ea.) green chiles, drained

1½ cups sharp natural cheddar cheese, shredded (6 oz.)
4 eggs, beaten
¼ cup flour
⅛ teaspoon Tabasco sauce (or more)
1½ cups milk

Brown the beef and onion together in a heavy skillet, separating with a fork to break up lumps. Drain off the fat. Sprinkle the meat with the salt and pepper. Halve the canned chiles lengthwise and remove the seeds. Place half of the chiles at the bottom of a 2-quart casserole or souffle dish. Cover with half the grated cheese. Next, put in the meat mixture. Arrange the remaining chiles over the meat. Combine the remaining cheese with the beaten eggs, flour, Tabasco and the milk. Beat this mixture until smooth, then pour it over the chiles. Put the container into your crockery pot slow-cooker, cover and bake on LOW for 5 hours, or until a knife inserted at the center comes out clean. Cool for 5 minutes before serving.

Old-Time Saloon Tomato Salad (4)

Serves 4

2 large beefsteak tomatoes
1 cup extra-dry white wine

4 tablespoons grated Parmesan cheese
4 tablespoons light olive or salad oil

Core the tomatoes and cut them into wedges. Put the wedges into a deep bowl and pour the wine over them. Let them marinate in the refrigerator for at least 10 minutes. Sprinkle the tomato wedges with the cheese and oil, then toss very lightly. Chill in the coldest area in your refrigerator for 45 minutes or more before serving.

Hungarian Cucumber Salad (4)

Serves 6

2 large cucumbers
½ cup vinegar
½ cup water
1 tablespoon sugar
½ teaspoon salt
⅛ teaspoon pepper
1 tablespoon fresh dill, chopped (optional)

Slice the cucumbers very thin, using a vegetable peeler or the cutting blade on a grater. Combine the vinegar, water, sugar, salt, pepper and dill in a bowl and marinate the cucumber slices at least one hour at room temperature. Marinating overnight greatly enhances the flavor. But there you have to make a choice: Many gourmets say the cucumber slices should be limp, but if you prefer crisper slices, marinate the vegetables in the refrigerator overnight.

Bean-Asparagus-Grape Salad (4)

Serves 4 to 6

½ lb. green beans (or 1 pkg. whole frozen beans)
1 lb. asparagus (or 2 boxes frozen)
1 lb. white grapes
1 head lettuce (Boston, iceberg, or leaf)
Juice of 1 lemon
2 tablespoons vegetable oil
½ cup heavy cream
½ teaspoon salt
⅛ teaspoon pepper
¼ teaspoon sugar

Cook the beans only until just tender, then rinse them at once in cold water to prevent further cooking. If you use fresh asparagus, tie it in 4 to 5 bunches and remove about half of each

148

stem, then cook in a quart of salted water. If using frozen asparagus, cook according to package directions—but not quite as long. Refrigerate the cooked vegetables. Pull the grapes from the stems. Break the lettuce into bite-size pieces and put into a salad bowl. Put the asparagus and beans over the torn leaves. Garnish with the grapes. Combine the lemon juice, oil, cream, salt, pepper and sugar into a dressing. Mix thoroughly and pour this dressing over the salad.

California Caesar Salad (4)

Serves 8

1 head lettuce
1 head romaine
2 eggs, coddled (1 minute)
½ teaspoon pepper (ground fresh)
1 tablespoon worcestershire sauce
6 anchovies (chopped)
½ teaspoon prepared mustard
¼ cup grated Parmesan cheese
½ cup French dressing (see recipe)
1 cup garlic croutons

Wash and dry the lettuce and romaine well. Break them up into a large salad bowl. Open the coddled eggs into a separate bowl and add the pepper, worcestershire sauce, chopped anchovies, mustard, cheese and French dressing. Combine these ingredients thoroughly and pour the mixture over the salad greens. Add the croutons and toss gently.

Vegetable Platter (4)

Serves 8

1 large head of lettuce
½ lb. zucchini, sliced
2 white turnips, sliced very thin
1 head cauliflower (in flowerets)
1 bunch celery, sliced
4 green onions, chopped

1 bunch carrots, cut in strips
3 tomatoes, cut in wedges (or 1 box cherry tomatoes)
2 green peppers, sliced
1 bunch parsley (or watercress)
½ cup French dressing (see index)

Wash and dry the lettuce leaves, but do not tear them up. Instead, line a platter with leaves, arranged face up like cups. Arrange the other vegetables in the lettuce cups, putting contrasting colors next to each other. Use the parsley (or cress) to fill in where you need a darker green and around the edges. Pour the dressing over the salad platter just before serving.

Wilted Lettuce Salad (4)

Serves 4

4 slices bacon
⅓ cup sugar
½ teaspoon salt
½ cup vinegar

2 hardcooked eggs, coarsely chopped
2 heads soft lettuce (or dandelion greens)

Dice the bacon and fry it in a skillet until crisp. Remove the bacon and reserve it until later. To the bacon drippings in the pan, add the sugar, salt, vinegar and ¼ cup water. Bring this mixture to a boil. Tear the greens in pieces and put them into a salad bowl. Pour the hot dressing over the greens and toss. Crumble the reserved diced bacon and sprinkle it and the chopped eggs over the top. Toss again, gently, and serve.

Spinach & Bacon Salad (4)

Serves 6

2 lbs. fresh spinach
3 hardcooked eggs, chopped

8 slices crisp bacon, crumbled
⅓ cup French dressing (see index)

Wash and dry the spinach leaves thoroughly. Remove stems and all wilted leaves. Break the spinach into bite-size sections and put them into a salad bowl. Sprinkle the hardcooked eggs and the bacon over the spinach. Pour on the French dressing and toss gently.

Greens & Mushroom Salad (4)

Serves 6

1 head romaine
1 bunch leaf lettuce
½ lb. endive

½ lb. fresh mushrooms
½ cup lemon French dressing (see index)

Wash and dry the romaine and lettuce leaves. Tear them into bite-size pieces and put them into a suitable bowl. Wipe the mushrooms and trim off the stem ends. If the mushrooms are discolored, peel them. Slice them thin—stems and crowns—and put them on top of the greens. Pour the lemon French dressing over and toss gently.

Romaine Salad Bowl (4)

Serves 6

2 heads romaine
2 bunches leaf lettuce
2 peeled tomatoes, cut
  in wedges
1 peeled cucumber,
  sliced
1 peeled avocado, sliced

6 green onions,
  chopped
⅓ cup French dressing
  (see index)
½ teaspoon dry
  tarragon (or
  chervil)

Tear the romaine and lettuce leaves into bite-size sections and put them into a salad bowl. Add the tomatoes, cucumber, avocado and onions. Toss salad with the French dressing and tarragon.

Endive Salad (4)

Serves 4

1 lb. endive
Green lettuce
  leaves

¼ cup French dressing
  (see index)
1 hardcooked egg,
  chopped

Wash the endive thoroughly and remove all wilted leaves. Cut the heads lengthwise into quarters and arrange them on the green lettuce leaves on a suitable platter. Shake the dressing to mix it well (or stir). Pour the French dressing over the endive and garnish the salad with the chopped egg.

Spinach-Lettuce-Onion Salad (4)

Serves 6

1 lb. spinach
1 head lettuce
1 can (3½ oz.)
  French-fried onions

½ cup French dressing
  (see index for
  recipe)

Wash the spinach well and take out the wilted leaves and all the stems. Dry it between paper towels, then break it into bite-size pieces. Break up the lettuce also and combine the spinach and lettuce in a suitable bowl. Heat the onions and arrange them over the top of the salad. Be sure dressing is well-mixed, then pour over the salad.

Gelatin Salad (4)

Serves 6

2 pkges. unflavored gelatin
2 cups hot water
2 cups beer
1½ tablespoons horseradish

½ cup finely chopped green onions (or chives)
½ cup finely chopped cucumber, drained

Dissolve the gelatin in the hot water completely. Cool and refrigerate. When the gelatin begins to jell, add the beer and horseradish. Beat well. Refrigerate once more. When the gelatin is about half congealed, add the onions and chopped cucumber. Return the salad to the refrigerator until it is firm and ready to serve.

Sicilian Tomato Salad (4)

Serves 4

1 lb. firm plum tomatoes
1 clove minced garlic
1 teaspoon dry basil (or 1 sprig fresh basil)

Salt and pepper
¼ cup light olive or salad oil
1½ teaspoons mild wine vinegar

Chill the tomatoes very well. When they are cold, slice them thin and place them in a serving bowl. Add the minced garlic. Crumble the dry basil between the palms of your hands and drop

it in (or chop the fresh basil very fine and add).
Sprinkle the tomatoes with salt and pepper. Pour
the oil and vinegar over this salad, and allow it to
marinate in the refrigerator for 15 minutes or
more before serving.

Beet Salad (4)

Serves 6

6 cooked beets (or 2
  medium cans),
  drained
Watercress, finely cut

French dressing (see
  index)
Lettuce leaves

Chill the beets in your refrigerator for several
hours, then cut them into thin slices. Combine
the beet slices with an equal amount of finely cut
watercress. Mix lightly with French dressing.
Serve on lettuce leaves in individual bowl or
plates. Or mound on crisp lettuce leaves and arrange around your entree on a large platter.

Cheddar Triangles from Austria (4)

Serves 6

6 slices firm white
  bread
¾ cup beer
3 eggs
5 oz. Cheddar cheese,
  grated

2 teaspoons ketchup
2 teaspoons flour
1 teaspoon paprika
4 tablespoons butter or
  margarine

Soak the bread slices in the beer on both sides.
Beat the eggs and add to them the cheese, ketchup,
flour and paprika, mixing well. Melt the butter in
a heavy skillet. Spread half of the cheese mixture
on one side of the bread. Place the bread (cheese
side down) in the skillet and fry it until golden
brown. Spread the slices on the unfried side with
the cheese mixture and turn the bread to brown

on the second side. Cut each slice into four triangles and serve hot.

Chutney Cheese Spread (4)

Makes about 1⅔ cups

2 pkges. cream cheese (3 oz. ea.), softened
1 cup shredded sharp natural Cheddar cheese
½ teaspoon curry powder

2 tablespoons beer
¼ teaspoon salt
¼ cup finely chopped chutney
1 tablespoon finely chopped green onion tops (or chives)

Combine the cheeses and blend them well. Add the curry powder, beer and salt, mixing well. Stir in the chutney. Chill for several hours in your refrigerator. Pour into a serving bowl and top with the green onions. If the mixture is too thick, thin with extra beer. Serve with crackers and fresh fruit as a dessert.

Dill Dip (4)

Makes about ⅔ cup

1 pkg. cream cheese (3 oz.)
1 tablespoon finely chopped green olives
⅛ teaspoon salt

1 teaspoon grated onion
¼ teaspoon dried dill weed
1 or 2 tablespoons beer

Soften the cream cheese and stir it well. Add the olives, salt, onion and dill weed. Mix well and stir in 1 tablespoon of beer. If this dip is not of satisfactory consistency, add the second tablespoon of beer—or even a little more. Serve it with celery or carrot sticks, potato chips, crackers, etc., as an appetizer.

Andalusian Gazpacho (4)

Serves 4

I love Gazpacho. It's a cold soup that is made in a blender. If it is made right, you will taste it for hours afterward and enjoy every memory. But don't think of it as a soup—think of it as an appetizer that will start any dinner off with a bang. Especially if it's a Spanish-style dinner.

5 large ripe tomatoes, peeled and seeded	⅓ cup olive or salad oil
6 small green peppers, peeled and seeded	¼ cup wine vinegar
2 cloves garlic	Salt
1 slice stale Italian or French bread	Croutons

In your electric blender, puree the tomatoes, peppers and garlic together. Soak the bread slice in water until it will absorb no more, then remove and drain it. Add the bread to the blender and combine it thoroughly with the tomato mixture. Put the mixture into a large bowl or pitcher and chill it for 3 to 4 hours. Then add the oil, vinegar and 1½ cups of water. Add salt to taste. Cover the bowl or pitcher and set it in your refrigerator for 4 or 5 hours more. When ready to serve, pour it into chilled bowls and top each bowl with croutons. If you like, an ice cube may be added to each bowl to keep the Gazpacho as cold as possible.

CHAPTER SEVEN
BREADS, CAKES AND PUDDINGS

Not all crockery pot slow-cookers will hold all baking containers and molds—not even where different makes are rated at the same capacity. Some cookers are oval and will not accommodate large round pans, some are squat and will not receive tall tube pans. Then, of course, a 3½-quart cooker will not hold the same volume as the larger capacity cookers, nor will it accommodate the same diameter pans. So, you may have to tailor some of these recipes down from the 4½-quart capacity size for which they were created, both in volume of ingredients and to fit your baking containers.

Measure your cooker's inside dimensions carefully for circumference and height, and note any taper from top to bottom circumferences. You want pans which will fit down to the bottom, or else sit on a trivet with space below and around, *not* tightly against the sides.

Once you have these dimensions, you can shop hardware, variety, gourmet shops, or the manufacturer of your cooker, for adequate-size baking containers: molds, with or without covers (you can make covers from aluminum foil); casseroles, if you can find the type with handles that don't prevent them from fitting into your cooker; bundt pans; tube pans; springform pans—or make your own from coffee or vegetable tins.

These bread and cake recipes were developed for the 4½-5 quart crockery pot with approximately 9¼-inch diameter and a 4-inch depth. It holds a great selection of 8-inch round pans—tube pans or springforms—9-cup bundt pans, souffle dishes up to 2-quart capacity, as well as a 2-pound coffee can, two 1-pound coffee cans, three 1-pound vegetable cans, or a 9-cup mold.

Please follow the directions carefully, especially where trivets are specified, or water for steaming, or foil for extra heating, or paper toweling to absorb excess steam. Also, do not remove the cover from the cooker at any time during the first two hours of baking.

To determine whether a bread or cake is done, use the toothpick test: Insert a wooden toothpick at the center of the bread or cake; if it comes out clean, the baking time is over.

Anadama Batter Bread (2)

Makes 2 small loaves

1 cup water
3 tablespoons shortening
¼ cup light molasses
2¾ cups sifted flour
½ cup cornmeal or oatmeal
2 teaspoons salt
1 pkg. dry yeast
1 egg

In a small saucepan, combine the water, shortening, and molasses, stir well and heat to 120 degrees Fahrenheit. Mix the flour with the oat- or cornmeal. In a mixing bowl, put 1½ cups of the flour mixture, the salt and the yeast. Mix well, then add the warmed liquid and the egg. Mix at medium speed for about 3 minutes, scraping the bowl from time to time. Use a slotted mixing spoon to stir in the remaining flour, beating and stirring until the batter is smooth. Grease two 1-pound coffee cans. Divide the batter between them and stand the cans upright in your crockery pot slow-cooker. Put 5 or 6 thicknesses of paper toweling over the mouth of the cooker and set the cover lightly on top. Bake on HIGH for 3 hours. Turn the loaves out on a rack to cool, laying the loaves lengthwise on the rack.

To make one large loaf, double the amounts of ingredients and follow directions for mixing. Then spray the inside of your crockery pot slow-cooker with lecithin, or grease it, shape the dough into a round loaf, set it into the cooker, cover the mouth with paper toweling and set the cover on top. Bake on HIGH for 3 hours.

Buttermilk Bread (2)

Makes 2 small loaves

½ cup buttermilk	1¼ teaspoons salt
½ cup water	2 tablespoons sugar
2 tablespoons butter or margarine	¼ teaspoon baking soda
3 cups flour	½ cake yeast (or 1½ teaspoons dry yeast)

In a saucepan, heat the buttermilk, water, and butter to 120 degrees Fahrenheit. In a large mixing bowl, mix together 1 cup of the flour, the salt, sugar, soda, and yeast. Add the warmed liquid and beat at the mixer's medium speed for 2 or 3 minutes. Add the remaining flour gradually, mixing with a slotted spoon, until the batter pulls away from the sides and bottom of the bowl. Divide the batter between 2 greased 1-pound coffee cans. Stand the cans upright in your crockery pot slow-cooker. Cover the top of the cooker with 5 or 6 layers of paper toweling and set the cooker's cover in place. Bake on HIGH for 3 hours. Cool for 5 minutes, then turn out of cans and let cool in a horizontal position on a cooling rack.

To make a large loaf of this bread, double the amount of ingredients and follow directions for mixing. Then spray the inside of the cooker with lecithin, or grease it well, shape the dough into a round loaf, set it in the crockery pot, cover with paper toweling and the top, then bake on HIGH for 3 hours.

French Bread (2)

Makes 1 loaf

This bread is not like the very white commercial "French bread" without substance we usually buy. Baked in a crockery pot slow-cooker, it more closely resembles authentic French bread which is baked with unbleached hard-wheat flour in an oven where it is surrounded by heat—substantial and crusty.

1½ cups water	1 tablespoon sugar
4 cups sifted flour	2 teaspoons salt
1 cake yeast	

Heat the water to 120 degrees Fahrenheit. In a large mixing bowl, put 1 cup of the flour, the yeast, salt and sugar. Pour the heated water into the flour mixture and beat at medium speed until the batter is smooth. Add 1 cup of flour at a time, mixing with a slotted spoon. Add only enough flour until the batter pulls away from the sides and bottom of the bowl. Then transfer the batter to a floured board and knead in the rest of the flour until it is no longer sticky—about 5 to 8 minutes. If you are using a 3½-quart crockery pot slow-cooker, shape the dough into a ball to fit, spray the inside of the cooker with lecithin, place 4 or 5 thicknesses of paper toweling over the mouth, and set the cover on top. Cover and bake on HIGH for 3 hours. If you are using a 4½-quart or larger cooker, put the dough into a 1½- or 2-quart greased souffle dish or casserole and bake on HIGH, after installing paper toweling and the top, for 3 hours.

Old World Rye Bread (2)

Makes 1 large loaf

2 cups rye flour	1½ cups water
¼ cup cocoa	¼ cup molasses
2 cakes yeast	2 tablespoons butter or
2 teaspoons salt	margarine
2 tablespoons caraway seed	¼ cup brown sugar, packed firmly
2½ cups white flour (or whole wheat)	Corn meal

In a large mixing bowl, combine the rye flour, cocoa, yeast, salt, caraway seed and 1 cup of the white or whole wheat flour. In a small saucepan, warm to 120 degrees Fahrenheit the water, molasses, butter and brown sugar. Pour the heated mixture into the flour mixture and beat until smooth. Transfer the dough to a floured breadboard and knead in the remaining 1½ cups of flour. Knead for 8 to 10 minutes—until the dough is firm and elastic. Spray your crockery pot slow-cooker with lecithin or grease it well. Sprinkle corn meal on the bottom. Shape the dough into a round loaf and place it directly into the cooker. Cover the mouth of the cooker with 4 or 5 layers of paper toweling and cover with the cooker lid. Bake on HIGH for 2 hours. Test with a wooden toothpick for doneness. Let the bread cool uncovered in the crockery pot for 5 minutes, then turn it out onto a rack to cook completely.

Swedish Beer Rye (2)

Makes 1 large loaf

1¾ cups beer	2 teaspoons salt
¼ cup water	3 cups rye meal or
¼ cup brown sugar	flour
¼ cup molasses	3 cups white flour
⅓ cup butter	1 tablespoon caraway
2 cakes yeast	seed

In a small saucepan, combine the beer, water, brown sugar, molasses and butter. Heat to 120 degrees Fahrenheit, stirring to mix the sugar and molasses. The butter need not melt completely over the heat. In a large mixing bowl, combine the yeast, salt and 1 cup each of the rye and white flour. Add the heated mixture and beat until smooth. Add the remaining flours and beat together until well mixed. Turn the batter into a well-greased 2-quart casserole or souffle dish, then place the container into your crockery pot slow-cooker. Place 5 or 6 layers of paper toweling over the mouth of the crockery pot and put the cover over them. Bake on HIGH for 3 hours. Allow the bread to cool in its pan for about 5 minutes, then turn it out on a rack to cool completely.

This bread is equally delicious when made with ½ cup of brown sugar instead of ¼ cup each of molasses and brown sugar.

Cinnamon Coffee Bread (2)

Makes 1 loaf

1 pkg. dry yeast
¼ cup warm water
  (105-115 degrees F.)
⅔ cup buttermilk
1 egg
2¾ cups flour
¼ cup soft butter or
  margarine
¼ cup sugar

1 teaspoon baking
  powder
1 teaspoon salt
¾ cup sugar
1 teaspoon cinnamon
½ cup finely chopped
  nuts
½ cup melted butter or
  margarine

Dissolve the yeast in the warm water in a large mixing bowl. Add the buttermilk, egg, 1¼ cups of the flour, the ¼ cup of soft butter, ¼ cup of sugar, 1 teaspoon of baking powder and 1 teaspoon of salt. Blend for 30 seconds with the mixer on low speed, scraping the sides and bottom of the bowl. Then beat for 2 minutes on medium speed. Stir in the remaining flour (the dough should be soft and slightly sticky). Knead for 5 minutes, or about 200 turns, on a lightly floured board. Cut the dough into 1- to 2-inch sections. Form each piece into a ball. Combine the ¾ cup sugar, 1 teaspoon cinnamon and ½ cup of finely chopped nuts. Melt the ½ cup of butter. Roll each ball in the butter and then in the sugar-nut mixture. Place a layer of balls in a well-buttered bundt pan (9-in.), so they barely touch. Space successive layers in the same manner. Pour any remaining butter and sugar-nut mixture over the top. Place the bundt pan in your crockery pot slow-cooker and cover. Allow the cake to rise until doubled, approximately 45 minutes. Then cover the opening of the crockery pot with 6 thicknesses of paper toweling and place the cover lightly on top, allowing a slight opening for the escape of excess steam. Bake on HIGH for 3 hours. Remove from the pan and allow the cake to cool on a rack.

Cinnamon Raisin Bread (2)
Makes 1 loaf

2 pkges. dry yeast	1 teaspoon cinnamon
½ cup warm water (105-115 degrees F.)	2 tablespoons wheat germ
1 teaspoon salt	2½ cups flour
2 tablespoons honey	1 cup raisins
4 tablespoons oil	

In a medium-size mixing bowl, dissolve the yeast in the warm water. Add the salt, honey, oil, cinnamon, wheat germ and 1 cup of the flour. Beat well. Add the raisins and another cup of flour, and blend well. Spread the remaining half cup of flour on the bread board and turn out the dough. Knead for about 5 minutes. Set into a buttered 1½-quart casserole or a 6-cup baking mold. Allow the dough to rise until doubled. When doubled, put the bread into your crockery pot slow-cooker and cover the top first with 4 to 6 thicknesses of paper toweling, then the cover, allowing a slight opening for excess steam to escape. Bake on HIGH for 3 hours. Turn out on a wire rack to cool completely. This bread slices well when cold, especially with a serrated-edge knife. It is delicious toasted and buttered.

Zucchini Bread (2)

Makes 1 loaf

3 eggs
¾ cup salad oil
2 cups (1 lb.) raw zucchini, peeled and grated
1 tablespoon vanilla
3 cups sifted flour
1 teaspoon salt
1 teaspoon baking soda
½ teaspoon baking powder
1 tablespoon cinnamon
½ cup broken pecans or almonds

Beat the eggs until light and foamy. Add the oil, zucchini and vanilla, mixing well. Combine the flour, salt, soda, baking powder and cinnamon. Add to the egg mixture, stirring until all ingredients are well-mixed. Fold in the nuts. Pour into a lightly greased and floured 9-cup bundt pan. Pour 2 cups of hot water into your crockery pot slow-cooker. Place trivet inside and put the cake pan on the trivet. Put a sheet of aluminum foil across the top of the crockery pot and set the cover firmly on top of the foil. Set the temperature control to HIGH and bake for 3½ hours. Test with a wooden toothpick for doneness. The pick will come out clean. The top will still look very moist. Allow to cool for 10 to 15 minutes before removing from the cake pan. This is a very moist and delicious bread which stays fresh for many days. Serve thin slices with cream cheese. It may be frozen and stored in your freezer.

Brandied Fruit Cake (2)

Makes an 8-inch cake

The recipe for this cake—and the original starter mix—was given to us by our good friend and neighbor Joyce Gordon, who had an idea it would work out well in a crockery pot slow-cooker. Boy, was she right! We classify it here as a short-time baking recipe but you'll need a week or more to make up the starter and ferment it to the right point. However, it's simple to do—and very much worth your while!

1 cup light raisins	¼ teaspoon salt
1 cup sugar	⅓ teaspoon nutmeg
1 cup water	1 teaspoon cinnamon
¼ lb. (1 stick) butter or margarine	1½ cups brandied fruit starter (see following recipe)
2½ cups flour	
¼ teaspoon ground cloves	1½ cups broken nutmeats
1 teaspoon baking soda	

Combine in a saucepan the raisins, sugar, water and butter. Boil for 1 minute. Remove from the heat and let cool. Sift together the flour, cloves, soda, salt, nutmeg and cinnamon. Mix the cooled ingredients with the dry ingredients. Add the brandied fruit starter and the nutmeats and mix well. Pour the batter into a well-greased 9-cup bundt pan. Put the pan into your crockery pot slow-cooker, place 4 or 5 layers of paper toweling over the top opening, and cover the pot. Bake on HIGH for 3½ hours. Cool for 5 minutes in the bundt pan before turning the cake out onto a cooling rack. This cake should be on the dry side when done and, like all fruit cakes, will taste even better the second day, or the third day—if it lasts that long. Maybe you ought to make several?

Brandied Fruit Cake Starter (4)

Makes 5 cups

5 cups canned fruit, drained (pineapple tidbits; canned cling peaches, diced; maraschino cherries, cut in half— combined in any proportion you prefer)
5 cups sugar
¾ teaspoon yeast

Combine the drained and cut-up fruit with the sugar and yeast. Let stand until the sugar and yeast dissolve. Pack into a clean glass container, cover loosely and store in a cool place for at least 1 week before using.

Only 1½ cups of this brandied fruit are required for a brandied fruit cake. The rest of the starter is to be used as a base and replenished regularly until required for more cakes. Mix the extra starter with 1 cup of any of the fruit used originally, or 1 cup of each fruit, and put it into another clean glass container. The juice of the fruit may be included at the time of replenishing but should be drained off later and used as a base for fruit punch. The starter should be replenished every two weeks. Otherwise you will have to make fresh starter a week before you make brandied fruit cake every time.

Cinnamon Rolls (2)

Makes 1 dozen

1 pkg. dry yeast
¼ cup warm water
(105-115 degrees F.)
⅔ cup buttermilk
1 egg
2¾ cups flour
¼ cup soft butter or
margarine

¼ cup sugar
½ teaspoon baking
powder
1 teaspoon salt
1 tablespoon soft
butter or margarine
¼ cup sugar
1 teaspoon cinnamon

Dissolve the yeast in the warm water in a large mixing bowl. Add the buttermilk, egg, 1¼ cups of the flour, ¼ cup butter, ¼ cup sugar, the baking powder and salt. Blend for 30 seconds with your mixer on low speed, scraping the sides and bottom of the bowl. Then beat for 2 minutes at medium speed. Stir in the remaining flour (the dough should be soft and slightly sticky), knead for 5 minutes (about 200 turns) on a lightly floured board. Roll out the dough into a 12- by 7-inch rectangle and spread it with the 1 tablespoon of soft butter. Combine the last ¼ cup of sugar and the teaspoon of cinnamon, then sprinkle this mixture over the dough. Roll up, beginning at the wide side, and seal well by pinching the edge of the dough roll. Cut across into 12 slices. Place these slices in a greased 8-inch round layer cake pan, not touching. Place the cake pan in your 4½- or 5-quart crockery pot slow-cooker, cover, and let the rolls rise until doubled. Place 5 or 6 thicknesses of paper toweling over the mouth of the cooker and set the cover on top of them lightly, leaving a small opening for steam to escape through. Bake on HIGH for 3 hours. Remove the hot rolls from the pan and allow them to cool on a rack.

Pecan Rolls (2)

Makes 1 dozen

1 pkg. dry yeast	1 teaspoon salt
¼ cup warm water (105-115 degrees F.)	1 tablespoon soft butter or margarine
⅔ cup buttermilk	¼ cup sugar
1 egg	1 teaspoon cinnamon
2¾ cups flour	¼ cup melted butter or margarine
¼ cup soft butter or margarine	¼ cup brown sugar, firmly packed
¼ cup sugar	½ cup broken pecans
½ teaspoon baking powder	

Dissolve the yeast in the warm water in a large mixing bowl. Add the buttermilk, egg, 1¼ cups of the flour, ¼ cup soft butter, ¼ cup sugar, the baking powder and the salt. Blend for 30 seconds with the mixer on low speed, scraping the sides and bottom of the bowl, then beat for 2 minutes at medium speed. Stir in the remaining flour (the dough should be soft and slightly sticky). Knead for 5 minutes, or about 200 turns, on a lightly floured board. Roll the dough into a 12- by 7-inch rectangle, and spread it with the tablespoon of soft butter. Combine the ¼ cup sugar and the teaspoon of cinnamon and spread or sprinkle it over the butter. Roll up, beginning at the wide side. Seal well by pinching the edge of the dough. Cut across into 12 slices. Coat an 8-inch round baking pan with a mixture of the ¼ cup melted butter, ¼ cup brown sugar and ½ cup broken pecans. Lay the rolls on top of this mixture. Place cake pan in crockery pot slow-cooker, cover, and allow rolls to rise until doubled. Place 5 or 6 thicknesses of paper toweling over top of pot and cover lightly, allowing a slight opening for steam to escape. Bake on HIGH for 3 hours. Cool for about 10 minutes, then turn out on rack.

Carrot Cake (2)

2 eggs
1 cup brown sugar, packed
¾ cup salad oil
1½ cups flour
¾ teaspoon baking soda
⅛ teaspoon salt
1 teaspoon baking powder
1 teaspoon cinnamon
1 cup raw carrots, finely grated
½ cup chopped nuts
½ cup raisins

Beat the eggs until creamy, then gradually add the sugar, beating until the batter is smooth. Gradually beat in the oil. Combine the flour, soda, salt, baking powder, cinnamon and add the dry mixture to the batter, beating until well-blended. Add the carrots, nuts and raisins, mixing well. Pour into a 2-lb. coffee can or a 6-cup mold, well-greased and floured. Cover the container tightly with aluminum foil. Pour 2 cups of hot water into your crockery pot slow-cooker. Place the cakepan inside on a trivet. Cover the crockery pot and bake on HIGH for 2½ to 3½ hours, or until a toothpick tests clean at its center. Cool for at least 10 minutes on a rack before turning out onto a cake platter.

Honey-Carrot Cake (2)

Makes an 8-inch cake

2 cups sifted flour
1 teaspoon salt
2 teaspoons baking powder
1 teaspoon baking soda
1½ teaspoons cinnamon
½ teaspoon nutmeg
½ teaspoon ginger
⅓ cup butter or margarine
½ cup honey
2 eggs
2 cups carrots, finely grated
¼ cup orange juice
1 teaspoon vanilla
1 cup golden raisins, chopped

172

Sift together the flour, salt, baking powder, baking soda, and the cinnamon, nutmeg, and ginger. In a large mixing bowl, cream the butter until soft. Continue creaming the butter while adding the honey in a fine stream. Add the eggs and mix well. In another, small bowl, blend together the grated carrots, orange juice and vanilla. Add this to the creamed mixture and blend well. Add the flour mixture, beating only until well blended. Stir in the raisins. Turn the batter into a greased 9-cup bundt pan. Put the pan into your crockery pot slow-cooker. Cover the top with 4 or 5 layers of paper toweling and then the pot cover. Bake on HIGH for 3½ hours. Cool for 5 to 10 minutes in the cake pan before turning the cake out onto a cooling rack.

Liegnitzer Bomben [German Honey Cake] (2)

Makes an 8-inch cake

¾ cup sugar
¾ cup honey
3 tablespoons butter or margarine
4 eggs
½ cup cocoa
¼ teaspoon ground cloves
½ teaspoon cinnamon
¼ teaspoon nutmeg
⅛ teaspoon cardamom (optional)
¼ teaspoon allspice

¾ cup raisins (or currants)
¾ cup diced candied lemon peel, packed firmly
¾ cup almonds, chopped coarsely
3 tablespoons rum (or 1½ teaspoons rum extract)
1½ tablespoons baking powder
2¼ cups plus 3 tablespoons flour

Melt together the sugar, honey and butter over low heat, then cool. Beat the eggs until creamy and add the cocoa, cloves, cinnamon, nutmeg, cardamom and allspice. Mix well. Add the raisins, lemon peel, almonds and rum to the eggs. Add the cooled honey mixture and mix well. Combine the baking powder and the flour, then add the dry mixture gradually to the batter, beating until all ingredients are well mixed. This will be a heavy batter. Pour the batter into a well-greased and floured 9-cup bundt pan and place it in your crockery pot slow-cooker. Cover the mouth of the cooker with 5 or 6 layers of paper toweling and set the pot cover on top. Bake on HIGH for 2½ to 3 hours. Test with a toothpick after 2½ hours. Cool in pan for 5 minutes, then turn out on a rack. This cake may be glazed or sliced and served with butter or cream cheese.

Honey Cake (2)

Makes an 8-inch cake

2 tablespoons oil	1 teaspoon baking soda
1 cup sugar	¼ teaspoon salt
3 eggs	1 teaspoon cinnamon
1 cup cold strong coffee	¼ teaspoon ginger
1 cup honey	½ teaspoon nutmeg
3 cups sifted flour	½ cup raisins
2 teaspoons baking powder	½ cup nuts, coarsely chopped

Beat the oil, sugar and eggs together until light and thick. Combine the coffee and honey. Sift together the flour, baking powder, soda, salt, cinnamon, ginger, nutmeg. Add this mixture to the batter alternately with the coffee-honey mixture. Stir in the raisins and nuts. Pour the completed batter into a greased and floured 9-inch bundt pan. Place the cake pan into your crockery pot slow-cooker. Cover the top with four thicknesses of paper toweling and place the cover lightly on top, allowing opening for excess moisture to escape. Bake on HIGH for 4 hours. Cool cake for at least 10 minutes before removing it from the cake pan. This cake may be frosted with a standard powdered sugar frosting or served plain, sliced thin.

Apple Cake (2)

Makes an 8-inch cake

2 cups sugar	1½ teaspoons baking soda
1¼ cups oil	1 teaspoon salt
2 eggs	1 teaspoon cinnamon
1 teaspoon vanilla	½ teaspoon nutmeg
3 cups chopped apples	½ cup chopped nuts (optional)
3 cups flour	

Beat together the sugar, oil, vanilla and eggs until light and creamy. Add the chopped apples and mix thoroughly. Combine the flour, soda, salt, cinnamon and nutmeg and add them to the apple batter. Mix very well. Fold in the nuts and pour the batter into a lightly greased and floured 9-cup bundt pan. Place in your crockery pot slow-cooker and cover with 5 paper towels. Place the cooker cover over the towels lightly, allowing a small opening for excess moisture to escape. Cook on HIGH for 3 hours. Remove to a cake rack and cool for 10 to 15 minutes before turning out onto a cake platter. This cake may be served plain, with your favorite frosting, or with a warm caramel sauce (see the following recipe).

Warm Caramel Sauce for Apple Cake (4)

Enough for 1 cake

1 cup brown sugar
½ cup butter or
  margarine
2 tablespoons flour

2 teaspoons vanilla
1 cup sweet cream (or
  evaporated milk)

Combine the sugar, butter, flour, vanilla and cream in a saucepan. Simmer until thick, stirring occasionally.

Quick Apple Dessert (2)

Serves 4 to 6

1 pkg. yellow cake mix
  (single layer size)
1 can (3½ oz.) flaked
  coconut
½ teaspoon cinnamon

4 tablespoons melted
  butter or margarine
1 can (21 oz.) apple pie
  filling

Combine the dry cake mix, coconut, and cinnamon. Stir in the melted butter. Press ⅔ of the mixture into an ungreased 8-inch round cake pan. Spread with the pie filling. Crumble the remaining coconut mixture over the top. Place the cake pan in your crockery pot slow-cooker, put 5 thicknesses of paper toweling over the top, and then set the cover over lightly, allowing a slight space for the escape of excess steam. Bake on HIGH for 2½ to 3 hours. This desert may be served hot or cold—even topped with ice cream!

Bot-Bo Fahn [Chinese Steamed Rice Pudding with Preserved Fruit] (2)

Serves 6 to 8

3 cups cooked rice
¼ cup sugar
¼ cup butter or margarine

Assorted sweet preserved fruit*
Almonds

Combine the cooked rice (made with 1 cup raw rice) with the sugar. Using the full ¼ cup of butter, grease a 1½-quart baking dish. Arrange a layer of preserved fruit and almonds in the bottom of the dish, then cover with a layer of the rice. Repeat layers until the baking dish is full, ending with a layer of rice. Pour 2 cups of hot water into your crockery pot slow-cooker and place a trivet in it. Place the baking dish on the trivet, cover the pot, and cook on LOW for 2 hours. Serve hot.

*Note: Chinese preserved fruits are preserved with sugar and honey, some flavored with licorice or cloves, others with ginger. You will usually find in Chinese markets (and in some super markets featuring Oriental delicacies) such delicious things as: sugar-preserved winter melon, clove-flavored plums, glazed orange rind, preserved kumquat, dried litchi nuts, preserved *wongpay* (yellow skin), and spiced ginger. Domestic glazed fruit, such as cherries, citron, lemon, orange, etc., may be substituted in a pinch—but the result would not be truly Chinese.

Pastry Crust Dough (4)

Makes one 9-in. crust

1 cup flour
1/4 teaspoon salt
1/4 cup butter or
    margarine

1 1/2 tablespoons vegetable
    shortening
3 tablespoons cold
    water

Into a mixing bowl, sift the flour and salt together. Cut in the butter and the vegetable shortening until the mixture looks like coarse meal. Add the water and blend it in quickly, using a tossing motion. Press the dampened particles together into a ball of dough. Roll it out on a floured board into a circle about 1/8-inch thick and 2 inches larger than the diameter of the pie pan. Fold the dough in quarters and place it in the pan if it is to be a bottom crust, or over the pan if it is to be a top crust. If a filling is to be baked in the shell, bake according to the recipe. If the crust is to be baked first, prick the bottom and sides with a fork to prevent puffing and fit a slightly smaller pan into the crust. This recipe is included here as a top crust for pot pies or steak and kidney pie. Fit it in place and crimp or flute the edges to hold it sealed. Bake according to the recipe. If you need more crust, double the recipe but only use about 5 tablespoons of cold water.

INDEX